FROM T

'A CATHEDRAL!

Fancy

A

Cuppa?

NORTH
YORKSHIRE

Matador
9 Priory Business Park
Kibworth Beauchamp
Leicestershire LE8 0RX, UK
Tel: (+44) 116 279 2299
Fax: (+44) 116 279 2277
Email: books@troubador.co.uk
Web: www.troubador.co.uk/matador

ISBN 978 1783064 823

British Library Cataloguing in Publication Data.
A catalogue record for this book is available from the British Library.

Typeset by Troubador Publishing Ltd, Leicester, UK

Matador is an imprint of Troubador Publishing Ltd

Printed and bound in the UK by TJ International, Padstow, Cornwall

For my wife, Anita,
so she knows what I was up to while she was at work.

CONTENTS

FOREWORD

As we're based in North Yorkshire, you'd think a tour of the county's main towns and villages would be quickly done, but far from it.

North Yorkshire is the biggest county in England and it's over 100 miles from one end to the other. It's also surely one of the most beautiful counties, with vast variations between coastal resorts like Filey and Scarborough, fishing villages like Staithes, and rural market towns dotted across the county. 40% of the county's land mass is National Park, taking in the North York Moors and the Yorkshire Dales.

And there's so much history to the area. We all know about Richard III's Yorkshire connections, but how many knew that William the Conqueror's son was born in North Yorkshire? Or that Roman roads criss-crossed the county, with York a central hub? But there are also extraordinary pre-Roman connections to North Yorkshire, which we discovered on this tour, the most notable of which appears on no map in print today!

I've taken a broad definition of North Yorkshire in deciding which 50 towns, villages and cities to visit. This means that I have included York, Middlesbrough, Redcar and Yarm, which are part of what's called the 'ceremonial county' rather than officially within the North Yorkshire local government boundaries.

For each place visited, I provide a short introduction, picking out a coffee or tea connection if there is one. And if not, I include any quirky fact that caught my eye during my stay.

But I also gave myself some flexibility, by choosing not to visit places like Acomb (a York suburb), Norton (so close to the food capital – Malton) and Loftus (I preferred Staithes). So, if you have a favourite place for a cuppa in any of those three, do let me know, and I'm sorry I missed it!

Coffee and tea

A lot of foodie writers as well as coffee or tea reviewers assume that the best venues are down in London, or at a pinch in the northern urban centres of Leeds, Manchester, Newcastle or Liverpool.

The great pleasure in doing this tour of North Yorkshire was to discover that it really is possible to find top quality coffee, tea AND cake away from the big university towns or cities.

Sure, York and Harrogate probably do have the best of what we're looking for in the *Fancy a Cuppa?* guidebooks. But it's great to see how easy it is to find excellent quality in market towns, and even sometimes in small villages. The taste for good coffee and tea has spread…

I don't limit myself to what the coffee experts call 'third wave' coffee shops. We do have some of these in North Yorkshire, though I hate the term (and prefer to call them 'artisan' coffee shops, if they must have a label). But my aim was to find the best there was in every town (even if not in all the villages).

As for tea, it does not HAVE to be loose leaf to make it into my reviews, but it really is preferable, and judging by the number of tea rooms that do manage to provide good quality loose leaf, I have to wonder why more places don't. There are lots of ways of serving this now without creating massive washing-up hassles afterwards. If you're running a tea room and only serve tea bags, do visit some of the venues I review here and see for yourselves how it can be done!

Finally, I have kept the reviews very brief. The aim is that this should be a guidebook to carry round with you on your travels, rather than an academic tome weighing you down.

For most towns, I aimed at two venues, usually one specialising in tea and the other in coffee. In some, I only found one that felt good enough to review; in others, Harrogate especially, there were simply too many to review all the great places for a good cuppa, so kept the entries to a maximum of three.

Tour de France and Cleveland Way

If you're up in North Yorkshire for the Tour de France, or following the route after the peloton has been and gone, there are around 20 coffee shops and tea rooms featured here that are on the route, across 11 towns and villages on that Leeds to Harrogate stage. Many other venues are within a few miles of the Tour route.

If on the other hand, you prefer to keep fit by walking, and like to avoid the crowds, maybe the Cleveland Way is for you. Again, there are around 20 venues in the 10 towns and villages along that 110 mile route from Helmsley to Filey.

Fancy a Cuppa?

Fancy a Cuppa, North Yorkshire? is the 4th tea and coffee guide to come from the *FancyaCuppa?* team. It follows on from our joint first effort, reviewing 50 great tea rooms and coffee shops in the UK, all with a story to tell; the second book, based on our tour of 26 US states in search of good tea and coffee; and last year's epic odyssey round 89 UK cathedral towns and cities, finding great places for a cuppa.

I hope you find this guide both useful and enjoyable, but most of all, I hope it proves a help in steering you towards that all important cup of tea or coffee, wherever you are in God's Own County.

SOME FAVOURITES

North Yorkshire towns/villages with historical tea/coffee connections

Leyburn – *Had an annual tea festival in Victorian days; shame it can't be revived today…*

Settle – *A gatekeeper would provide hot water for tea to day-trippers picnicking in town in the old days.*

Robin Hoods Bay – *In the 18th century, tea would be smuggled in from the Netherlands.*

Easingwold – *The engine on the local railway line in the 19th century was called 'T'awd Coffee Pot'!*

Saltburn – *What's now a contemporary bistro looking out over the beach was once a splendid tea room.*

North Yorkshire's pre-Roman history spots

Feizor – *One of the finds of our tour, the Celtic Wall appears on no map. It's a 1 mile hike from the tea room. Sceptics say there's no proof this wall is ancient, but we like to believe it is…*

Lord Stones – *An ancient stone circle a few hundred yards from the coffee shop with views down to Teesside.*

Boroughbridge – *Enormous standing stones on the edge of town. One is bigger than any at Stonehenge.*

Bentham – *The Big Stone stands right on the Lancashire border, one of a line apparently naturally formed.*

North Yorkshire's American connections

Filey – *One of the big battles involving John Paul Jones during the Wars of Independence took place off the coast at Filey. Was our tea room owner's great great grandfather there to witness the battle?*

Tadcaster – *The Pilgrim Fathers are thought to have met in the beautiful building that now houses the local Council staff. Shame THIS can't be a tea room...*

Ripon/Selby – *The Washington family arms are to be found in stained-glass windows in Ripon Cathedral and Selby Abbey.*

North Yorkshire's Australian connections

Great Ayton – *They may have moved Captain Cook's childhood home to Melbourne (and put a plinth in its place), but Great Ayton still has a rather unique statue of Cook as a skinny 16 year-old on the village green.*

Staithes – *Where Captain Cook had his job in a grocer's shop. Trouble is the cottage he lived in here was swept away in a storm. There's a replica in its place now.*

Whitby – *The town usually associated with Cook. His monument stands looking down over the harbour, where he first boarded a ship.*

Stokesley – *Jane Pace, the first white woman to settle in Victoria, came from here, and her house in North Yorkshire is still remembered with a plaque on the outside.*

Skipton – *Wes, the guy who made the Top Ten in the 2013 UK barista championships, runs the coffee shop in Skipton, but honed his skills living Down Under!*

North Yorkshire's literary connections

Malton – *It is thought that Charles Dickens' brother had an office above our favourite tea room in Malton, so you may be following in his footsteps if you have a cuppa upstairs.*

Filey – *Bramwells Tea Room is most definitely NOT named after the Bronte brother (that was Branwell), even if one of his sisters lived across the road…*

Ingleton – *Arthur Conan Doyle's Mum lived round here, as did a Sherlock family, and a nearby village is called Holmes. I'll let you deduce the rest…*

Scarborough – *Anne Bronte is buried here, though the blue plaque marking where she lived is misleadingly placed on the wall of the Grand Hotel. She was here before that grand edifice was built! Alan Aykbourn's plays have premiered in Scarborough 75 times.*

Thirsk – *Home of the real James Herriot, Alf Wight. I don't think he ever had time for a tea break, though…*

The venues

Top 5 coffee destinations

York – *Spring Espresso and the two Perky Peacock branches lead the way (and many recommend Harlequin too).*

Harrogate – *Fantastic coffee capital of North Yorkshire, with the three venues reviewed here (LMDC, Hoxton North, Bean & Bud) and two others we didn't find room for (Rasmus, Baltzersens).*

Malton – *Supposed to be Yorkshire's food capital, but ex-barista champion Simon has a top spot for coffee in Leoni.*

Skipton – *Wes at Bean Loved was one of the top 10 UK baristas in 2013. Great coffee shop all round.*

Ripon – *Oliver's Pantry have set the bar so much higher for tea or coffee in Ripon – and kept great connections to the past occupiers of their building!*

Top 5 tea rooms

Francis Tea Rooms – Scarborough: *Great tea in an extraordinary setting; quality all round and great value.*

Black Swan Tea Rooms – Helmsley: *Blending and branding their own tea now. This is an elegant hotel tea room, but bikers in leathers are just as welcome as families in their Sunday best.*

Olde Young Tea House – Middlesbrough: *Still one of my favourite vintage chic tea rooms.*

SkyBlueRed Studio – Guisborough: *Great to see a non-profit social enterprise can serve up tea of this quality in a wonderful atmosphere.*

Lavenders Tea Room – Thornton-le-Dale: *For a lesson in how to mix quality with old and modern, this is the place: contemporary décor; 14th century building; great loose leaf tea.*

(and running them close: Luby's Tea Room in Cross Hills; The Mill Race in Aysgarth)

Top 5 venues for cake

Tea-Hee in Easingwold – *A personal touch to every cake we ate; there's a surprise in every bite!*

Frumenty & Fluffin in Ingleton – *Extraordinary cakes: the black forest scones were unforgettable!*

Spring Espresso in York – *Their signature cake (apple, pecan, bourbon chocolate cake) can't be beaten.*

Olde Young Tea House in Middlesbrough – *Just go to her Facebook page for the pic of her daily cake.*

Tea Lounge in Tadcaster – *Roll on the day when Lisa publishes those recipes passed down from her Granny!*

Top venues with a view

There are two categories here: coastal views and Dales views

On the coast for sea views you can't beat:-

– Tides in Sandsend near Whitby
– Swell Café in Robin Hoods Bay
– Camfields in Saltburn
– Seasons Café in Redcar
– Sea Drift Café in Staithes

For views of the Dales over your cuppa:-

– 1897 Coffee Shop in Hawes
– Muker Tea Room
– Ivy Cottage Tea Room in Reeth

Tea/Coffee Shop buildings with unusual uses in the past

Perky Peacock in York – *This tower on the Ouse was a toll point and the place where dead bodies used to be hauled out of the water* (below the coffee shop level and many years ago…).

Francis Tea Room in Scarborough – *Was a 1940s ladies hair salon, with private cubicles still in place today for taking tea.*

Swell Café Bar in Robin Hoods Bay – *Was a Wesleyan Chapel in the 18th century and can still be hired for weddings today.*

Oliver's Pantry in Ripon – *This was an old ginger beer bottling factory once upon a time. They still have bottles to prove it!*

Rural Arts Café in Thirsk – *Housed in Thirsk's old court house.*

Joe Cornish Gallery Café in Northallerton – *Housed in Northallerton's old Registry Office, built in the 1730s.*

More top buildings housing a coffee shop or tea room in North Yorkshire

The Mill Race Tea Room in Aysgarth – *This former mill sits right over the wonderful Aysgarth Falls.*

Lavenders Tea Room in Thornton-le-Dale – *Built in the 14th century, this former forge is probably the oldest building housing a tea room in this book.*

The Black Swan Tea Rooms in Helmsley – *This 16th century hotel has had its share of celebrity guests over the years, from William Wordsworth to members of the Royal Family.*

Seasons Café in Richmond – *This is inside Richmond's old railway station, now converted to a community hub, but you may well be taking tea on one of the old platforms.*

Muker Tea Rooms – *This was once the residence of the village vicar, but he was moved some years ago when the property was condemned as uninhabitable; you'd never believe it now this beautiful tea room is there.*

THE COFFEE LOVERS' GUIDE TO NORTH YORKSHIRE – FAVOURITE ROASTERS

Grumpy Mule	Lord Stones near Chop Gate
	Number 50 in Haxby
	Muker Tea Room
	Mocha in Richmond
	Oliver's Pantry in Ripon
	Bean Loved in Skipton
Limini Coffee	Number 5 Coffee House in Great Ayton
	Bexters Tea Room in Stokesley
Lincoln & York	Penny Bank Café in Kirkbymoorside
Masteroast	CoffEco in Grassington
	Leoni in Malton
Monmouth Coffee	Cotton House in Helmsley
Nude Espresso	Hoxton North in Harrogate
Origin Coffee	Perky Peacock in York

PJ Gourmet (Peter James)	Roasters in Scarborough
	Perky Peacock in York
Railtown Coffee	Olivia's in Northallerton
Rounton Coffee	Joe Cornish Gallery in Northallerton
Square Mile	LMDC in Harrogate
	Spring Espresso in York
Workshop Coffee	Hoxton North in Harrogate
York Coffee Emporium	Whistle Stop Café in Bedale

Some venues, such as Bean & Bud in Harrogate are constantly rotating their roaster so not listed here. And coffee shops do also switch suppliers, so we can't guarantee this list is still accurate today.

THE TEA LOVERS' GUIDE TO NORTH YORKSHIRE
– FAVOURITE BLENDERS/SUPPLIERS
– LOOSE LEAF ONLY

Brew Tea Co.	1897 Coffee Shop in Hawes
	Hoxton North in Harrogate
Canton Tea Company	Spring Espresso in York
Coopers	Penny Bank Café in Kirkbymoorside
Cygnet Teas	Black Swan Tea Rooms in Helmsley
Drury Tea & Coffee	Luby's Tea room in Cross Hills
Holmfirth Tea	Bexters Tea Room in Stokesley
Jeeves & Jericho	Oliver's Pantry in Ripon
Jenier World of Teas	SkyBlueRed Studio in Guisborough
Leaf Shop	The Sitting Room in Saltburn
Newby Teas	Sugar Mouse in Easingwold
Northern Tea Merchants	Tea-Hee in Easingwold
Suki Teas	Tea-Hee in Easingwold
	CoffEco in Grassington
	Seasons Café in Redcar; and in Richmond
	Bean Loved in Skipton

Taylors of Harrogate	China Blue in Knaresborough
	Posthorn Tea Room in Leyburn
	Hidden Monkey Tea Room in Malton
	Bettys in Northallerton
	Cafe Cocoa in Pickering
	Tea Parlour in Middleton near Pickering
	Three Sheep Tea Room in Skipton
	Lavenders Tea Room in Thornton-le-Dale
Tregothnan Tea	The Mill Race in Aysgarth
Trumpers Tea	Bean & Bud in Harrogate

We had excellent loose –leaf tea at the following tea rooms but didn't find out who supplied them!

Francis Tea Rooms in Scarborough
Botham's of Whitby
The Hairy Fig in York

AYSGARTH

As soon as the Tour de France published the Yorkshire stages for the 2014 race, cyclists began to try their luck on the hills and climbs the professionals would be doing in July. Aysgarth is slap-bang in the middle of that route.

Most visitors come to visit the beautiful series of waterfalls just half a mile out of the village. Unlike the falls in Ingleton (also in this book), the Aysgarth Falls are free to see. And they are quite spectacular, especially after heavy rain.

This is classic James Herriot country. But a whole range of artists have been inspired by the Aysgarth countryside, from Wordsworth to Turner and on to the director of *Robin Hood: Prince of Thieves*!

Mill Race Tea Shop

A rare chance to taste Tregothnan tea – grown in Cornwall and loose leaf, of course. Sit and watch the river flow past this 1780s mill house, then stand on the bridge and admire the beautiful Aysgarth Falls. Cake recommendation: Black Sheep (that's the local beer) and Chocolate. House speciality: Cheese Lovers Afternoon Tea (Wensleydale scones, tea loaf, gingerbread, a wedge of Wensleydale and a pot of tea).

Aysgarth Falls DL8 3SR
Tel: 01969 663 446
http://www.themillraceteashop.co.uk/

Opening hours

10.00am – 5.00pm Daily in spring and summer
Weekends only in autumn/winter
Closed December till Boxing Day

More tea – in the village itself

Hamilton's Tea Rooms

Right on the Tour de France route in 2014. If you're reading this before July, here's where you can sit and sip your Yorkshire Tea while watching the peloton race past. In Victorian days, this was a hardware shop in a busy village centre; it's now a beautiful B&B where you can have a cuppa with the house speciality: Wensleydale cheese scones, shortbread or their daily home-made soup – all made in-house.

Yoredale House, Aysgarth DL8 3AE
Tel: 01969 663 423
www.yoredalehouse.com

Opening hours

9.30am – 4.30pm Monday
(10.00am – 4.00pm in winter)
Closed Tuesdays
9.30am – 4.30pm Wednesday – Sunday
(10.00am – 4.00pm in winter)

BEDALE

Highlight of Bedale is surely the volunteer-run Wensleydale Railway station, where steam trains and old diesel locomotives stop on the run from Leeming Bar to Redmire. Very handy for our top tip for coffee or tea in Bedale, which is right in the old station building!

Bedale rose to national fame a few years ago when the Bedale Community Bakery featured on a reality fly-on-the-wall TV series; it's still going strong next door to the petting farm near the Station – great bread.

A more gruesome memorial is the Leech House, down by the river, where local doctors would store leeches until they were needed for 'bleeding' a patient. It's now a listed building.

Coffee?

Whistle Stop Café

Best coffee in Bedale, supplied by York Coffee Emporium. Teas here are good, too, from the Metropolitan Tea Company. Come at the right time of year and you may get a cake with plums picked from the tree at the front of the station! The steam and diesel trains go past all year round, though there's much more chance of seeing a train at the peak of the summer season.

Station House, The Craft Yard, Bedale DL8 1BZ
Tel: 01677 426 446
Facebook: The Whistle Stop Cafe Bedale Station
@whistlestop123

Opening hours

9.00am – 5.00pm Monday – Saturday
(earlier closing in winter)
10.00am – 3.00pm Sunday

BENTHAM

Bentham's biggest attraction is The Big Stone. It's actually up on the moors two miles out of town. It stands about 10 yards from the Lancashire border, but it's a natural formation, not placed here to keep out the Red Rose. There are steps up it and locals apparently used to picnic on top of the stone on fine days.

Bentham may be a border town but it somehow never got involved in any fracas between the Red and White Roses. The biggest battles are probably during the rush hour these days, when none of the roads seem wide enough for two vehicles to pass at any one time.

Coffee or tea?

37 Main Street

Best coffee in Bentham. Beans roasted by Farrers, over the border in Lancashire. They also do cream teas. Sit in the front room and watch the world go by or go to the room out the back, where you'll not only have a nice cosy fire to sit by in winter, but you also get to watch owner Denise at work in the kitchen area. A freshly-baked sponge cake was just coming out of the oven during our visit.

37 Main Street, High Bentham LA2 7HQ
Tel: 01524 263150
Facebook: 37 Main Street

Opening hours

9.30am – 4.30pm Monday – Saturday
Closed Sundays

BOROUGHBRIDGE

The Devil's Arrows are three standing stones on the outskirts of Boroughbridge. Are they part of an enormous stone circle from the Bronze Age? Or do they line up for one of those summer solstice moonlight effects? Whatever the real story is, they're worth a visit – one is taller than Stonehenge.

Isabella Bird is a woman after the *Fancy a Cuppa?* heart. She lived for a while in the Manor House on the main square, but her 19th century travels ranged from Hawaii to Afghanistan – surely a film of her life would be an epic…

This was a 'new town' in Norman times, built on the Great North Road, a mile or so from the 'old' Aldborough (with the best Roman remains in Yorkshire – but only open weekends). Once upon a time, there would up to 2,000 cattle a day driven through Boroughbridge from Scotland.

Lots of bridges in town, with lots of history. Our favourite was built by Blind Jack of Knaresborough, though there's not even a plaque to remember his extraordinary work. Don't miss the flood marks in the Tourist Information Office – 3' deep in 1991!

Coffee?

The Old Foundry Kitchen

The stories this building could tell, from its days when it was part of the town's foundry to today's contemporary space recommended by NetMums as particularly child-friendly. There's a nice cup of coffee to be had, using a blend supplied by Coffee with Conscience (a Scottish-based fair-trade company) and fabulous cakes baked on-site. Don't miss the bridge behind the foundry, which some say was built from fragments of the 4th Devil's Arrows standing stone.

Foundry Yard, New Row, Boroughbridge YO51 9AX
Tel: 01423 324 173
www.oldfoundrykitchen.co.uk
@OFKitchen
Wifi available

Opening hours

9.00am – 5.00pm Monday – Friday
9.00am – 4.00pm Saturday
Closed Sundays

Tea?

Bowe and Co

Chances are, as you pour your tea or milk, the tea pot or milk jug you're using was made by owner Liz. Cakes and scones are all made in-house, too. And you'll get a little jelly baby with your pot of Yorkshire Tea (or one of the other coffees and teas supplied by Taylors of Harrogate). There's a warm, friendly feel to this place right on the High Street. And look out for the photo of Liz from (some) years ago, when she met Princess Diana – but that was before her tea room days!

27 High Street, Boroughbridge YO51 9AW
Tel: 01423 323 037
http://boweandco.com/
@boweandco

Opening hours

8.00am – 5.00pm Monday – Friday
8.00am – 4.30pm Saturday
Closed Sundays

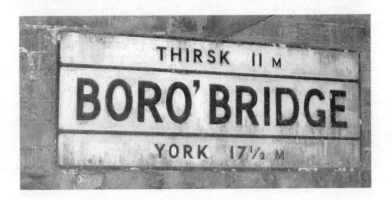

CHOP GATE

There isn't much in this village, but as a child I loved it just for the fact that it is pronounced 'Chop Yat', due to its Viking origins.

The coffee shop is a three mile climb out of the village, high up on the edge of the Moors. Lovely walks around here (on the Cleveland Way) and beautiful views.

The Lord Stones are a half ring of standing stones high up on the Moor with views down to Teesside and up to the North York Moors. Nobody knows what they were for or when they were built...

Coffee?

Lord Stones

Coffee next to one of the hidden secrets of ancient North Yorkshire – the Lordstones are just a short stroll from this coffee shop, which is three miles from Chop Gate. The Grumpy Mule coffee is excellent, the cakes pretty good, too. And don't miss the deli here, where you can find produce from the farm next door. If you have meat in your sandwich, you can be sure it's fresh and not had far to come from farm to fork. This place was completely refurbished in 2013, when the three brothers who run the neighbouring farm and sporting estate took it on.

Lord Stones Country Park, Carlton Bank, Chop Gate
TS9 7JH
Tel: 01642 778 482
www.lordstones.com

Opening hours

9.00am – 5.00pm Daily
(And restaurant open some evenings also for meals)

CROSS HILLS

This village is a little North Yorkshire outpost very close to the Lancashire and West Yorkshire borders. There's a constant flow of traffic passing through all day between Nelson and Colne in Lancashire and Keighley in West Yorkshire. Skipton is just a few miles to the north, though, and you can spot the Dales from the cross roads.

The Cross Hills settlement grew around the local post office for the neighbouring village of Glusburn. Cross Hills feels like a small town, though, with independent butchers, estate agents, even a school of dance and of music! Oh, and a tea room…

Luby's Tea Room

Owner Luby's creative mind designed the amazing interior of this beautiful tea room. There are lots of sweets and toys to draw the kids in, and if it's just a little bit too girly for some boys, there's some rather cool mushroom seats out the front to sit and have your tea or soft drinks. Top quality loose leaf tea supplied by the excellent Drury Tea & Coffee in London. The cakes and scones are all home-baked, and everything is served on vintage bone china. Top tip, if they have any: the ginger sponge (fantastically moist, with slithers of real ginger through it).

33 Main Street, Cross Hills BD20 8TA
Tel: 01535 631 110
Facebook: Luby's Tea Room and Gift Emporium

Opening hours

10.00am – 4.30pm Monday – Saturday
(open till 5pm Friday)
Closed Sundays

14

EASINGWOLD

'T'Awd Coffee Pot' was the steam engine that used to run on the short stretch of track that made up the Easingwold Railway until 1957. Before the railways, Easingwold was the first horse-change on the York to Newcastle stagecoach route.

It's now one of North Yorkshire's more affluent market towns, with beautiful Georgian houses dotted along its main streets. But pop into the parish church, and you'll find the only intact 'poor coffin' in England; it was used for burials of those who could not afford their own resting place.

Just by the priest's entrance to the parish church is Ann Harrison's grave. Known as Nana Ran Dan, she 'was chaste but no prude', and she ran a pub here in the 18th century. Local legend has it that if you run round the grave three times at night, you'll see her re-appear.

The message carved in stone above the library door (this was the local school in Victorian Easingwold) is 'Learn or Leave'. Next door is now a beauty salon, but it was once the police station, and it still has the old cell door at the front. No bad hair days here, then!

Coffee or tea?

TeaHee Cheesemonger & Espresso Bar

It's quality all round in this excellent venue housed in the town's old tollbooth. If you like family connections, you'll love the fact that owner Sophie's uncle ran a tea plantation in Papua New Guinea which still supplies the Northern Tea Merchants. You can have tea from them or from the excellent Suki Teas, or Coopers. This is also the best place for coffee in Easingwold (supplied by the Heavenly Coffee Company in South Yorkshire). And there's a personal touch to all the cakes, which are made in their kitchens upstairs. Our top tip, if they have it: the orange sponge or the cranberry and treacle tart. This is also a cheesemonger, so you know what to have in your sandwich!

3 Tollbooth Cottage, Market Place, Easingwold, North Yorkshire YO61 3AB
Tel: 01347 823 533
www.teahee.co.uk
@teahee

Opening hours

7.00am – 6.00pm Monday – Friday
7.00am – 5.00pm Saturday
Closed on Sundays

Tea?

Sugar Mouse

Owner Angela Spencer could probably tell a few gruesome tales from her time as the Yorkshire Post's crime correspondent. What a contrast it must be to bring smiles to the faces of children (and adults) at the sight of jar after jar of old goody favourites like Dolly Mixtures and Fizzy Wizzy. She serves up an excellent pot of loose leaf tea, too (from Newby Teas in London) and there are lots of home-made tray bakes and scones on offer. They also give you a couple of squares of fudge to go with your cuppa (we had the Yorkshire rhubarb fudge – fantastic!).

2 Central Buildings, Market Place, Easingwold, North Yorkshire YO61 3AB
Tel: 01347 822 818
www.sugar-mouse.co.uk
@mouseytweet
Facebook: Sugar Mouse Easingwold

Wifi available

Opening hours

9.30am – 5.30pm Monday – Saturday
Closed Sundays

FEIZOR

Feizor is only half a mile or so from the main A65, but take a five minute stroll out of the village and you're into some of the most spectacular Yorkshire Dales scenery, with craggy hill tops, limestone pavements and walking trails up to the Three Peaks.

The Celtic Wall does not feature on any printed map, and none of the walkers we met even knew it existed. It's only 20 metres or so long and it's perched up on top of a slope, some way off the beaten track, but this is an extraordinary piece of what is thought to be pre-Roman Yorkshire history. It's about a mile's hike up from the village and you'll need a stout pair of shoes to get there. SD802675 Grid Reference for those using an OS map!

Tea?

Elaine's Tea Room

This place is popular with walkers and cyclists, though owner Elaine says that in deep snow one year someone arrived for tea on skis. You'll get a good pot of Ringtons Tea here and some wonderful home-baked cakes either to set you on your way for a Dales walk or recharge those batteries after a long bike ride. Elaine began the tea room as a hobby to run alongside her husband's farming business over the road. She's gained such a reputation now though that she barely manages a day off. If you're keen to see the Celtic Wall near Feizor, go straight up the hill from the tea room, starting with a walk through the farmyard and carry on for about a mile before you scramble up a slope to the right of the path.

Home Barn, Feizor LA2 8DF
Tel: 01729 824 114
Facebook: Elaine's Tearooms, Feizor

Opening hours

9.00am – 4.30pm Daily (every day except Christmas Day)

FILEY

Filey is the place to come if you're a fan of John Paul Jones. That's not the singer; it's the American ship's captain who terrorised the British coast during the wars of independence in the 1770s. There's a memorial board at the spot where locals must have watched one of the big battles off the coast at Filey.

Filey's most famous street is The Crescent, which was built in the 1800s, but modelled on Bath's Georgian terraces. Actually, the best view of it on a clear day is from Filey Brigg, the promontory that sticks out into the sea to the north of town.

When the Romans built a signalling point on the Brigg, it was apparently 70m wide. Coastal erosion has whittled that down to barely a metre in places, but it's still a fantastic spot for fishing and bird-watching. It's also the end point of the 110-mile Cleveland Way, which begins in Helmsley.

Coffee?

Filey Bistro & Coffee Bar

Best coffee in Filey (from Seasons for Coffee, in West Yorkshire). This mother (Sue) and son (Martin) partnership set up shop here in February 2013. They rotate the tasks, one of them doing the cooking and baking one week, while the other works front-of-house, and then swap round the next week. They do a gluten-free carrot cake and chocolate cake, which is made locally, but the rest of the cakes and scones are made in-house. And if you stay for the evening, the bistro has regular themed tapas nights. Word has got around town that this is the place to come for a cuppa (and more) in Filey.

22 Murray Street, Filey YO14 9DG
Tel: 01723 512 032
Facebook: Filey Bistro & Coffee Bar LTD

Wifi available

Opening hours

8.00am – 5.00pm Monday – Thursday
8.00am – 7.00pm Friday-Saturday
9.00am – 4.00pm Sunday

Also open evenings from 6.00pm on Thursday – Saturday

Tea?

Bramwell's Tea Room

Owner Duncan's family goes back to his great-great grandfather who was a coble builder in the area in the 1700s – just think, he probably witnessed the great battle involving John Paul Jones, off the Filey coast. There's a lovely olde-worlde décor to this tea room, with china and teapots along the walls, old sewing machines up on high shelves and even a rack of clean white linen hanging above the counter! The Birchall Tea Rwandan blend makes for a good, strong brew, which goes down very nicely with the excellent home-baked cakes. And in case you're wondering about the name of the place: It was not named after the Bronte brother (even though Charlotte stayed across the road), who was Branwell, not Bramwell; it got its name because the previous owner liked the 1990s TV series, Bramwell, and the name has stuck!

33 Belle Vue Street, Filey YO14 9HU
Tel: 01723 513 344

No web presence

Opening hours

10.00am – 3.30pm Monday – Saturday
Closed Sundays

GARGRAVE

You can watch the narrow boats negotiating the lock as they take the big loop out of Skipton on the Leeds-Liverpool Canal. Apparently one local family still have a horse-drawn boat and can be seen sometimes in period costume alongside the canal walk.

The Romans crossed the river here via a ford, which was discovered a few years ago when they cleared the river base of plants. Sadly the Roman villa that was built nearby is no longer visible even in ruined form, and anyway it's now on private land.

Iain MacLeod, the former Chancellor of the Exchequer, who died very suddenly in 1970, is buried in Gargrave's main church cemetery. There's a blue plaque on the church entrance.

Tea?

White Cottage Tea Room

Owners Allan and Vicky used to work in the Lancashire textile industry, and they've used their eye for design and décor in refurbishing the interior of this beautiful 17th century cottage. Once you've negotiated the (very low) front entrance, your gaze will meet the lovely display of home-baked cakes from Yorkshire Curd tart and Bakewell to traditional sponge cakes. There are various options for afternoon tea, including a full slap-up high tea style for two, or the simpler Fireside Tea (cheese on toast followed by a piece of fruit cake). And you get a good pot of Yorkshire Tea to wash it all down. Delightful place.

5 West Street, Gargrave, BD23 3RD
Tel: 01756 748 229
Facebook: White Cottage Tea Room

Opening hours

11.00am – 4.30pm Monday
Closed Tuesday – Wednesday
11.00am – 4.30pm Thursday – Friday
10.00am – 5.00pm Saturday – Sunday

GRASSINGTON

One of the main centres of the Yorkshire Dales National Park, you're quite likely to find sheep wandering over the car park so mind how you drive round here.

This was a lead-mining centre once upon a time; the local museum is now housed in former lead miners' cottages on the main square.

Tom Lee was a local innkeeper in the 18th century, but he was also a highwayman, who is said to have murdered the village doctor. The doctor was about to denounce him, after all…

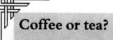

Coffee or tea?

CoffeEco

It's not often you get such a quality cup of coffee in a village coffee shop. But with their own blend roasted for them by Masteroast Coffee in Peterborough, and an espresso machine the owners went all the way to Verona to find for themselves, this is what you get at CoffeEco. Their tea is pretty good, too, coming loose leaf from Suki Teas. The '1641' engraved over the fireplace suggests this building has been around a while. The furthest they have managed to delve into its past though is when some of the older customers come with memories of buying their meat from the butchers in here. Owner Mark is one of those canny folk who got out of banking and insurance to feed his passion for coffee – on the evidence of this coffee shop, it was a good move!

6 Main Street, Grassington BD23 5AP
Tel: 01756 751 835
www.grassingtoncoffee.com
Facebook: Grassington Coffee

Wifi available

Opening hours

9.00am – 5.00pm Daily (closed Christmas Day)

GREAT AYTON

A pretty little village on the Captain Cook Trail. He went to school here before he got his first job working in Staithes. There's a museum now in his old school room and a statue of the young 16 year old Cook on the village green.

The house he lived in here has now been transported to Australia, and stands in a park in Melbourne! In its place is a ten foot tall monolith, with a plaque – from Australia – bizarrely noting the spot where he first sighted Australia. Bizarre because it's now in North Yorkshire...

Coffee?

Number 5 Coffee House

When owner Victoria was a little girl, this place was the village dairy. Now it's a thriving little coffee shop which welcomes all sorts, from groups of cyclists and walkers, to regulars and day-trippers on the Captain Cook trail. They use the excellent Limini Coffee here, roasted in Yorkshire; cakes and scones are all baked in-house, also using local ingredients where possible. And everything is beautifully-presented, from the latte art through to the little raspberry next to my coffee cake and the Number 5 painted in juice on my plate to remind me where I am. I'm rather glad Victoria left her career as a solicitor to take up baking and opened this lovely little coffee shop.

5 Park Square, Great Ayton, TS9 6BP
Tel: 01642 722 646

No web presence

Opening hours

Closed Mondays (except Bank Holidays)
10.00am – 4.30pm Tuesday – Saturday
Closed Sundays

GROSMONT

The village of Grosmont in the North York Moors grew up alongside the railway that linked Whitby to Pickering. So it's only right that the village should flourish even today from the steam trains that chug through the Moors on that same stretch of track. And Grosmont is home to the main engine shed for the Railway today, so railway enthusiasts flock here in their thousands.

If you're in the area, it's worth going a couple of miles beyond the next village – Goathland – to a one-mile stretch of Roman Road up on top of the moors. It's called Wheeldale Roman Road, with paving and ditches still visible (I'd have recommended a stop in Goathland, but I prefer the cafés and tea rooms in Grosmont!)

Old School Coffee Shop

Owners Bill and Emily have converted the old village school room into a wonderful cosy coffee shop, but what's nicest about their story is that in doing so they have recreated the space that was the original school room (for 111 pupils, indeed) when the place was built in the 1840s. And if the weather's nice, you can sit outside on a terrace that was the old school playground. They serve up the best coffee round this part of the Moors (from Coopers near Huddersfield). If it's tea you're after, they get theirs from the Kenyan suppliers Williamson Teas – all fair trade. And the cakes are so popular they have a special page on the website for their cake of the week.

Grosmont YO22 5QW
Tel: 01947 895 754
www.grosmontcoffeeshop.co.uk

Opening hours

Closed Mondays (except bank holidays and school holiday weeks)
10.30am – 4.30pm Tuesday – Sunday (4.00pm closure in spring & autumn)
Closed from November to February (but open for the February half-term week)

Tea?

Grosmont Station Tea Rooms

Fancy a strong pot of Yorkshire Tea and a slab of cake watching the steam trains chug past? This is a great place to do just that, but bear in mind that even when it's crowded, smut-covered train crew can jump the queue to get their flasks filled first. There are three cakes baked fresh every day. Apart from Carnforth Station itself, this is about as near as you're going to get in modern-day Britain to a *Brief Encounter* moment, though you're more likely to find lots of train spotters or families on one of the special themed weekends than you are a nervous couple on an innocent date. Great place to come for a cuppa and watch the steam trains chug past.

On the platform, Grosmont Station, Front Street, Grosmont YO22
www.nymr.co.uk

Opening hours

9.00am – 4.30pm Daily
(Basically opens just before first departure each day; and closes just after the last – so check the NYMR timetable for real opening hours)

GUISBOROUGH

The ruins of Gisborough Priory (yes, without a 'u') stand right in the centre of town. They are managed by English Heritage and there is a (small) fee to enter the grounds, but you can look down over them from the archway on the main road.

Guisborough's other visual highlight is the market 'cross', which is distinctive for having a weather vane and a sun dial rather than a cross on top. It is also missing the usual steps up to the stone plinth: these were apparently sold off in 1817, presumably in another period when public finances were stretched…

Virgo's Coffee Shop

This has been a café for some years, but one customer I spoke to knows the old lady who used to live here when this street was nearly all residential. Owner Helen Matthews has developed a menu with a focus on HALO (Healthy Eating and Light Option) and gluten-free. Top tip if it's available: a rather delicious orange and poppy seed cake with lemon icing – made from a recipe passed down the family through generations. And they served up the nicest coffee we found in Guisborough – roasted over the border in Lancashire, but they mix their own blend to make it unique to Virgo's.

25 Chaloner Street, Guisborough TS14 6QD
Tel: 01287 638 482
http://www.virgoscoffeeshop.co.uk/

Opening hours

9.15am – 4.00pm Monday – Saturday
Closed Sundays

Tea?

SkyBlueRed Studio

Fantastic loose leaf teas from Jenier World of Teas, based in Scotland, and cakes baked in-house which change with the seasons. Everything is served on beautiful vintage china. This not-for-profit tea room is a real hub of the Guisborough community now, with regular workshops in all sorts of crafts, their own kiln out the back for pottery parties and drop-in pot painting, and groups from across the town gathering here. Don't miss the photos of the building when Helen and others decided to convert what was a derelict shop into a wonderful workshop and tea room. Excellent initiative, great atmosphere, quality tea!

79-81 Church Street, Guisborough TS14 6HG
Tel: 01287 634 486
www.skyblueredstudio.co.uk
Facebook: Skybluered

Opening hours

10.00am – 4.00pm Monday – Tuesday
Closed Wednesdays
10.00am – 4.00pm Thursday – Saturday
Closed Sundays

HARROGATE

The HQ of Yorkshire Tea, our favourite tea to have at home, is just outside Harrogate, and is made by Betty's & Taylors of Harrogate.

There are lots of buildings harking back to Harrogate's heyday as a spa town: the Turkish Baths; the Royal Pump Rooms Museum (note the sulphurous smell outside the latter, though the tap on the outside doesn't seem to work anymore).

Wonderful green spaces, trees and flowers all through town. The Stray is a 200 acre area of common land. The street Stray Rein is where you could walk your animal…on a rein!

Grove House is an interesting place. It's where the Royal Antediluvian Order of Buffaloes is based these days, but was once the family home of Samson Fox, a former Mayor of Harrogate, whose descendants include the actors Edward and Emilia Fox.

Coffee?

LMDC espresso bar

You'd have to go a long way to find better coffee than Square Mile from London – made here on a beautiful Synesso machine. The standard cappuccino is just 6oz, but with quality like this, who needs more? The banana bread (great, toasted with butter) is made in-house; otherwise, the specialities are their brownies and blondies, baked by a local company just for LMDC. Those initials stand for the original name of the place: La Maison du Café. The building was once a coaching house, and they've exposed the old beams in the ceiling of the bar; great fresh feel inside and nice seats outside.

4 John Street, Harrogate HG1 1JZ
Tel: 07747 847834
www.lmdcespresso.co.uk
@lmdcespresso

Opening hours

8.00am – 4.00pm (but flexible) Daily

41

More coffee?

Hoxton North

With coffee from Workshop Coffee and Nude Espresso in London, and from Origin Coffee in Cornwall, this place will always have a great selection of quality brews to choose from. And if tea takes your fancy, they also have good loose leaf tea from the Brew Tea Co. Cakes are supplied by local independent bakers, including the wonderful ThatOldChestnut. Owners Tim and Vicky lived for over 10 years in the coffee shop-filled East End of London (around Hoxton, funnily enough), and decided to move back up north to bring a bit of that London life to Yorkshire. They've created a fantastic space right by the Harrogate Conference Centre in an old 1920s ladies fashion store.

52 Parliament St, Harrogate HG1 2RL
www.hoxtonnorth.com
@hoxtonnorth

Opening hours

Closed Mondays
8.30am – 5.00pm Tuesday – Friday
9.30am – 5.00pm Saturday
10.00am – 4.00pm Sunday

Coffee or tea?

Bean & Bud

Fantastic quality here in the venue which really pioneered Harrogate's independent coffee/tea scene. For coffee, they use around six roasters from around the country, with two different coffees to choose from at any one time. They had an excellent blend from Volcano Coffee and a single estate from Extract Coffee when we dropped in. Co-owner Ruth's knowledge of teas dates from her time working with Cafédirect and she's visited cooperatives in Africa and China (check-out their website for pics of her trip to Fujian Province, where she went to learn kung fu, but also came back with great tea connections). If you like a good, strong brew, try their English breakfast, supplied by Trumpers Teas (a mix of Assam, Ceylon and Kenya, including tea from growers Ruth has visited), or their Malawi single estate for something special. Great atmosphere here in a lovely street of independent retail outlets.

14 Commercial Street, Harrogate HG1 1TY
Tel: 01423 508 200
www.beanandbud.co.uk
@BeanandBud

Wifi available

Opening hours

9.00am – 5.00pm Monday – Saturday
Closed Sundays

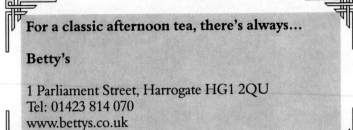

For a classic afternoon tea, there's always...

Betty's

1 Parliament Street, Harrogate HG1 2QU
Tel: 01423 814 070
www.bettys.co.uk

HAWES

Home of the Wensleydale Cheese (more on that in our tea review below), this town also brands itself as the 'Heart of the Dales'. Lots of winding cobbled streets, and views on all sides of classic Yorkshire Dales scenery.

It's also a bit of a living craft workshop, with rope-making still done down near the old railway station (there are plans to extend the Wensleydale Railway up this far one day), and a working cotton mill in the adjoining village of Gayle which dates from the 18th century.

Coffee?

Caffe Curva

Visited on their very first day of trading in October 2013. This place has moved Hawes into a better destination for coffee lovers, their coffee far better than anything else we tasted in town. Most of the cakes are baked in-house by owners Gino and Vanessa and you can watch them in action as you sip your coffee. Gino may have Italian roots, but the couple met in Nottinghamshire when working in education, so the move north is another example of coffee/tea shop owners who have gone for a complete change of career. They're keen walkers so they could hardly have picked a better spot than Hawes, and it's an indication of how well they've settled into Dales market town life that a friendly neighbour brought them flowers to wish them well on their opening day.

Market Place, Hawes DL8 3QZ
Tel: 07523 981 950
Facebook: Caffe Curva

Opening hours

Closed Mondays
8.30am (ish) – 5.00pm (ish) Tuesday – Sunday

Tea?

1897 Coffee Shop – Wensleydale Creamery

Excellent loose leaf tea from the Brew Tea Co. Served in a cafetiere style of pot so you need to let it brew (steep) a while before pouring if you like your tea strong! There's a great selection of cakes and scones, all baked in-house. Top tips: the paradise slice, the Eccles cakes, or a classic fruit cake with Wensleydale cheese. This place is special also for the stunning views out to the Dales or to a field of sheep grazing next door! It got its name from the year the first creamery was opened on this site. We don't normally recommend places set up to cater for tour groups or coachloads (this is probably the largest venue in the book), but the tea and cake beat the quality we found anywhere else in town, and there's something special about Yorkshire Wensleydale cheese and its place in the county's culture.

Gayle Lane, Hawes DL8 3RN
Tel: 01969 667 664
http://www.wensleydale.co.uk/places-to-eat

Wifi available

Opening hours

9.00am – 4.30pm Daily
Check the website for winter opening times

HAXBY

Haxby is actually a town, though there are days when it has more the feel of a retirement village or at best a dormitory for commuters to York, which lies five miles due south. There are certainly a lot of care homes in the area, with enough silver pounds to keep a couple of good cafés and a real bread bakery going.

Apparently there were Roman and Viking settlements here, though we found no trace of either on our brief visit. At least we did find good coffee…

Coffee?

Number 50

This used to be an old-fashioned tea room, popular with the residents of the local retirement homes. So it was a bit of a gamble when new owners Mike and Amanda decided early in 2013 that Haxby needed a contemporary coffee shop. Judging by the number of customers (of all ages) on the morning we were there, the gamble paid off. Quality sells. And the Grumpy Mule coffee makes for really good quality every time. They bake their own scones in-house and there were some impressive-looking sponge cakes on display, baked up the road in Malton. On fine days, there's a lovely garden out the back to sit and sip your coffee.

50 The Village, Haxby YO32 2HX
Tel: 01904 768 633
www.no50cafe.co.uk

Opening hours

8.00am – 4.00pm Monday – Friday
9.15am – 4.00pm Saturday
Closed Sundays

HELMSLEY

Come to Helmsley at the middle of the day on a summer's weekend and you're as likely to mix it up with 200 motor-cyclists as you are to bump into a coach tour or to be welcomed by walkers setting out on the 110-mile Cleveland Way around the North York Moors.

Turn up after 5pm or on a windy day in winter and you'll see the place for what it is: a charming, stone-cottaged market town, with beautiful gardens running down to the stream through town towards the river that marks Helmsley's boundary.

Walk to Rievaulx Abbey and you're doing the first two miles or so of the Cleveland Way; if you can't face that, there's a ruined Norman castle in town itself.

Coffee?

CottonHouse

They have the fantastic Monmouth Coffee from London here at CottonHouse so you're in for a treat if you haven't tasted it before. They make the cakes themselves, with gluten-free options, a rather tasty looking cinnamon and raisin bread, and freshly-baked brownies, which we watched going into the oven as we sat sipping our coffee. Owners David and Ruth moved up to Helmsley from Lincolnshire in 2012 when the opportunity arose to open up a coffee shop in this new build on the site of Helmsley's old stable yard. With the North York Moors National Park Authority based just up the road, it's no surprise that this whole new development blends in with the older local architecture – the beautiful, warm Yorkshire stone.

5/6 Barker's Yard, Borogate, Helmsley YO62 5BN
Tel: 01439 772 460
www.cottonhousehelmsley.co.uk
Facebook: CottonHouse

Opening hours

9.30am – 4.00pm Monday – Friday
10.00am – 4.30pm Saturday
11.00am – 4.00pm Sunday

Tea?

The Black Swan Tea Room

The Black Swan now have their own loose leaf tea company, producing the Cygnet Tea range, which goes from a basic Black Swan blend (a 'feel good tea'), through traditional Assam and Darjeelings to the more exotic white, green and oolong teas from China. They can match the teas to your mood, including their G & T tea, with juniper to cleanse your system, and the Whisky & Ginger tea to leave you 'mellow and content'. You can go for a full Afternoon Tea (with sandwiches, scones and patisseries) or just a simple cream tea with delicious home-made scones, jam and clotted cream. Everything is served on beautiful Wedgwood china and a tiered tray if you order the scones.

Parts of the Black Swan Hotel go back to the 16th century, though it only became a coaching inn when the 'Helmsley Highflyer' began operating in 1838 from York. Its residents over the years have included William Wordsworth and various members of the Royal Family. Down in the tea room, you'll get all sorts, from bikers in their leathers to elegantly-dressed families out for a Sunday treat. The tea room on the premises only opened in 2008, but with tea manager Alison Souter's passion and enthusiasm for all things tea-related, they are going from strength to strength.

Market Place, Helmsley YO62 5BJ
Tel: 01439 770 466
www.blackswan-helmsley.co.uk

http://www.blackswantea.co.uk/
@cygnettea

Wifi available

Opening hours

From 10.00am Daily

HOVINGHAM

One of the prettiest villages in North Yorkshire, it's all warm York stone buildings gathered around the very grand Hovingham Hall, linked today to the Duchess of Kent's family, but a few hundred years ago was the place where George III apparently learnt to ride a horse!

The Hovingham Spa train station was just on the edge of the village (you can just recognise the old station buildings, now a private residence) in the days when folk would come here to take the waters – the springs are in the grounds of Hovingham Hall, but there's still a lovely beck running through the village, with a ford, right in front of our venue for a cuppa…

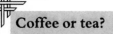

Coffee or tea?

Hovingham Spa Tea Rooms

This is an idyllic setting for a cuppa, with the pretty little beck flowing by, and a ford for cars to reach the cottages across the water. You'd never know that this was once the village garage, or that it was a funeral parlour before that. Owners Chris and Elaine have made it into a great little bakery and tea room (though we preferred the coffee – from Matthew Algie). There are excellent scones, Yorkshire curds and other cake delights. And these two are passionate members of the Campaign for Real Bread so try one of their door-step sandwiches with home-baked bread and ham off the bone.

Brookside, Hovingham, North Yorkshire, YO62 4LF
Tel: 01653 628898
No web presence

Opening hours

Closed Mondays (also Tuesdays in winter)
8.30am – 5.00pm Tuesday – Saturday
(Wednesday – Saturday in winter)
11.00am – 5.00pm Sunday

INGLETON

There are picture postcard views wherever you look in Ingleton, with its two rivers merging to form the River Greta, its railway viaduct and its narrow, winding streets up to The Square.

Sir Arthur Conan Doyle's Mum lived nearby; the Sherlock family was prominent in the area; and one of the villages a few miles away is called Holmes...

Lots of caving, walking, climbing round here, though we stuck to the swimming – in Ingleton's marvellous outdoor pool, built by local miners in the 1930s.

Coffee?

Seasons Cakes

Owners Daniel and Lesley have been baking great bread, pies and cakes for about eight years, but in 2013 branched out with this new bakery and coffee shop in Ingleton. Their Grand Milano coffee is the best brew we found in the village; they serve up Lichfields Tea, too. But it's their cakes and their sense of being a hub of the community that drew us in. Great fruit pies, vanilla slices, muffins, and you can see everyone at work in the bakery through the transparent screens to the shop.

The i Centre, Ingleton LA6 3BU
Tel: 01524 241 202
www.seasonscakes.co.uk
Facebook: Seasons Cakes

Opening hours

7.00am – 5.00pm Daily

Tea?

Frumenty & Fluffin

When Shirley and her daughter Lesley bought this place in 2009 it was in the old village bakery in the centre of Ingleton, so it's rather appropriate that they made it into a wonderful bakehouse. Lesley has trained as a patisserie chef, but they all get their hands in the cake mix and together produce a wonderful display of cakes and scones every day. There's a good mix of old-fashioned styles you don't often see any more like custard tarts and modern, quirky ideas like the black forest scone we tried. Everything served on elegant, but mix-and-match china. They've gone for a 1940s/50s feel to the place, but since most of the furniture and crockery is for sale, who knows how exactly it may look when it's your turn to visit! It'll still have that vintage feel, for sure. Tea is in tea bags, but with this quality of cake and that funky décor, we don't mind. Made a good pot, anyway!

15 Main Street, Ingleton, North Yorkshire LA6 3EB
Tel: 01524 241 659
Facebook: Frumenty and Fluffin
@frumentyfluffin

Opening hours

Closed Mondays
9.00am – 5.00pm Tuesday – Saturday
10.00am – 4.00pm Sunday

KIRKBYMOORSIDE

As its name suggests, this was originally a village ('By' is Danish) with a church on the edge of the moors. It's a town now, but that essentially is 'Kirkby' still today.

According to Wikipedia, it was the last town in England to introduce double yellow lines, and there are quite a few in view today, but you can park on the roadside cobbles as long as it isn't market day (Wednesday).

The George & Dragon and the Black Swan are wonderful old coaching inns. But it's the King's Head that has perhaps the best celebrity story: one of the Dukes of Buckingham whose family gave its name to the Palace in London had this house built and died there in 1687.

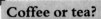

Coffee or tea?

Penny Bank Café

The Penny Bank was another name for the Yorkshire Bank when it first began trading in the 1860s. Since this building was once the Kirkbymoorside branch of that bank, it was a logical step for local couple Tony and Sheila to name their café the Penny Bank Café. They get their coffee from the excellent Lincoln & York (which is based, funnily enough, in neither city, but just south of the Humber). They also have a small range of loose leaf teas from Coopers (the basic English Breakfast is a good, strong Assam/Ceylon blend, but there's also Earl Grey, mint and green teas). Add in a moist piece of carrot cake (or any of the dozen or so other cakes) made in their own kitchens and you'll be tempted to go back for more, which a lot of the locals seemed to be doing anyway! And they use as much produce as they can from their own gardens at home (including making their own jams).

19 Market Place, Kirkbymoorside YO62 6AA
Tel: 01751 432 606
www.pennybankcafe.co.uk
@pennybankcafe1

Wifi available

Opening hours

8.00am – 5.00pm Monday – Saturday
10.00am – 3.00pm Sunday (winter)
9.00am – 4.00pm Sunday (summer)

KNARESBOROUGH

Ursula Sontheil is perhaps Knaresborough's most famous daughter. Better-known these days as Mother Shipton, her caves are now a tourist attraction by the river, but she is remembered for her 16th century visions of the future, having supposedly predicted the Great Fire of London, the Civil War, the victory over the Armada and much, much more.

Mother Shipton is one of seven characters painted onto Knaresborough's windows, high up above the various streets in the town centre (others include Guy Fawkes and 'Blind Jack', another local hero) – you can pick up a Town Windows Trail from the Tourist Info Office.

The town's annual Bed Race is just a bit of wacky fun, held every year since 1966 in June. It's helped them garner international links, though, to similar races in New Zealand and Germany.

Knaresborough's best views come from the 14th century castle, looking down over the River Nidd and the railway viaduct. And if you arrive by train, you have the unique experience of emerging from a tunnel on one side of the station and the viaduct on the other side.

The oldest chemist ('chymist') in England – opened in 1720 – is in Knaresborough's Market Place. You could try the tea rooms upstairs here, especially when our favourite venue is closed...

Tea?

China Blue Tearoom

It's rather nice that owner Amy should have opened this tea room in Jockey Lane, Knaresborough. She used to work full-time in the racing stables at Middleham, but had to stop after a riding accident. She's still very attached to her horses, so when the tearoom opens on a Saturday, you won't find her serving tea because she'll be out riding one of her favourite horses instead. Her Mum Doreen runs the tea room with her and takes charge of most of the baking. They get all their teas and coffees from Taylors of Harrogate, so you know the quality is good. We opted for a pot of Assam, which came loose leaf and was excellent. Lovely décor here, all shelves of blue china, with more out on a tray in front, and even an old milk churn, painted blue, of course, parked outside in the street.

18 Jockey Lane, Knaresborough HG5 0HF
No web presence

Opening hours

Closed Mondays
10.00am – 3.00pm Tuesday – Friday
10.00am – 2.30pm Saturday
Closed Sundays

LEYBURN

In the 1850s they used to hold an annual tea festival on Leyburn's Shawl, the bank of grass that looks out over the Dales below and beyond. What a shame it discontinued. The Shawl probably got its name from a Norse connection, but the legend goes that Mary Queen of Scots lost her shawl here when trying to escape from Bolton Castle nearby.

On the edge of town is a Tea Pottery, which has been making tea pots of all shapes, sizes and themes for nearly 40 years. You can watch them at work from the moulding through to the paintwork, and then have a pot of (Yorkshire) tea on the premises, before you purchase your pot.

Leyburn is one stop from the end of the Wensleydale Railway, so time your visit right and you'll spot a steam train (or maybe a diesel) chugging past on its way to or from Leeming Bar and Bedale.

Coffee?

Chambers Coffee House

This coffee shop is perfectly-placed in the middle of Leyburn's wide market place. With seating outside, you can watch the locals of Leyburn and the thousands of Dales visitors trail past on a fine day. Caffe Vinci does a decent cup of coffee and is certainly the best we found in Leyburn. Scones come fresh out of the oven in time for opening every day – delicious with butter or with jam and cream. Ruth, who runs the place now, worked here for two years before taking it on herself and she clearly loves it – no wonder, it's a popular place.

Central Chambers, Market Place, Leyburn DL8 5BD
Tel: 01969 625 919
www.chamberscoffee.co.uk

Wifi available

Opening hours

9.00am – 5.00pm Monday – Saturday
(closes 4.00pm in winter)
10.00am – 5.00pm Sunday

Posthorn Tea Room and Café

There are lovely displays of tea trays in the window, with a samovar and more bone china out towards the back room of this little tea shop on the market place in Leyburn. If you order the classic Yorkshire Tea, they'll serve it in a pot with tea bags. But if loose leaf tea is what you're looking for, don't miss out on the excellent range of teas on offer, also from Taylors of Harrogate. We had a fresh, light Ceylon Tea, one of several black tea options, but they are also developing their green, white and oolong collection if those are what tickle your taste buds.

This tea room was Tony Douthwaite's Mum's for nearly 20 years, but she has handed it on to him now. She keeps baking the amazingly good cakes and is slowly working on teaching Tony the secrets! Meantime, he hopes she'll carry on baking from her two home kitchens because nobody can match her skills. Top tips for cake: the ginger and date loaf was moist and fresh or the Old Peculier Fruit Loaf, served with Wensleydale Cheese. There's a full gluten-free menu, too.

Market Place, Leyburn DL8 5AW
Tel: 01969 622243

Opening hours

9.30am – 4.00pm Monday – Saturday
(until 5pm Easter – autumn half term)
10.00am – 4.00pm Sunday
(until 5pm Easter – autumn half term)

MALTON

The classic Yorkshire market town. Pick the right day and they'll be auctioning off the sheep and cattle just near the centre of town. Then wander down to the 'new' market place where you can buy all sorts of ropes or other hardware in a store that must have been there a few generations.

This has been a major crossroads since Roman times. Go to the Orchard Fields along the Old Malton Road for a sense of just how big the Roman fort was round here.

It's always been a horse-riding centre, too, starting with the Roman cavalry and now with lots of horse racing stables nearby.

Lovers of old independent cinemas should not miss the Palace Theatre and Cinema too – wonderful art deco interiors and a great programme of films on show.

Coffee?

Leoni Coffee House

This place has everything. Owner Simon Robertson was UK barista champion in 2002, 2003 and 2005, and came 8th in the world in 2005, too. But these days he's happy just providing the quality for his local community rather than proving himself on the world stage. Coffee roasted by Masteroast of Peterborough. But it's the talent of the baristas that makes it special. One of the best coffees we had in North Yorkshire. Cakes are good, too, mostly made in-house, but the chocolate cake and lemon drizzle come the Patisserie just up the street from here. There's also loose leaf tea on the menu if coffee isn't your cuppa.

Great atmosphere, too. There's a cheery welcome as soon as you walk through the door. And a cosy, intimate feel all over the two floors; lots of old library books on the walls, a bike hanging over the staircase, and even old coffee-making equipment dotted about the place. Nice historical touch too: Simon's great great grandfather owned the property when it was a butcher's shop a long time ago...

16 Wheelgate, Malton YO17 7HP
Tel: 01653 691 321
No web presence

Opening hours

9.00am – 5.30pm Monday – Saturday
Closed Sundays

Tea?

The Hidden Monkey Tea Rooms

There's lovely loose leaf tea from Taylors of Harrogate here. Or you can go for the basic Yorkshire Tea in a bag if that's all you want. Cream Tea is just over four pounds for a pot of Yorkshire and a scone with cream and jam. Or go for one of the delicious home-made cakes – on the day of our visit, there were five sponge cakes, scones, flapjacks and a gluten-free option. The homemade puddings look good too, if you're here for a full lunch.

This tea room got its name under the previous owner, after a visit to the Royal Yacht Britannia. Apparently the Royal Family play a game of find-the-monkey when on the yacht, so the idea was brought back to North Yorkshire, and you'll see a monkey hanging somewhere in the tea room even now! The building was once a ladies' outfitters – there are invoices pinned to the wall today. It is also thought that Charles Dickens' brother had offices upstairs here, so Dickens may well have popped in during a visit to Malton…

34 Market Place, Malton YO17 7LW
Tel: 01653 694 982
www.hiddenmonkeytearooms.co.uk

Opening hours

9.00am – 5.00pm Monday – Saturday
Closed Sundays

MASHAM

Old Peculier (not 'peculiar') is these days associated with one of Masham's local breweries – Theakston's. It was originally the name of the local consistory court, traditionally run by the Church, but under Henry VIII transferred to Trinity College, Cambridge – which explains why there are so many references to Trinity all over town!

Two breweries in town (Theakston's and Black Sheep) mean the chances are you'll have the warm, musty smell of hops filling the Masham air when you visit.

Masham is busiest around its Sheep Fair in late September. It began as a trade fair for the sheep from nearby Fountains or Rievaulx Abbeys, though these days you're more likely to find a visiting shearer from Down Under among the local farmers than you are a monk!

Coffee?

Johnny Baghdad's Café

'Johnny Bagdad' has been catering at music festivals for years and still does to this day. But when the opportunity came up to create a fixed coffee shop – with kitchens – on Masham's Market Place, he leapt at the chance. From the outside, you'd never know how funky and bohemian the internal décor is: picked up from travels around the Middle East, Central America, India, they make a fantastic space inside. Coffee is the best we found in Masham, making a decent cappuccino, and the home-baked cakes are delicious. Recommendation: the Chocolate & Guinness Cake or the Orange & Almond. This place actually specialises in its Middle Eastern lunchtime dishes (lamb or goat curry, couscous are favourites) but we stuck to the coffee and cake this time. Worth visiting, though, just for the wonderful décor!

52 Market Place, Masham HG4 4ED
Tel: 01765 688 809
http://suncatcherscafe.co.uk/johnny-baghdads/

Opening hours

10.00am – 5.00pm Daily

Tea?

Fancy That Tea Rooms

Owner Jamie is a qualified baker who took on this tea room about six years ago, and is now ably assisted in the kitchen by Hollie, who also gets her hands in the scone mix most mornings. Jamie lives upstairs and is very much part of the community, volunteering at the local fire station. Teas are all in tea bags, but Taylors of Harrogate makes up for that with good quality. Cakes and scones are all baked in-house, most of them by owner Jamie, who's been baking for years – and it shows in the quality. Nicest place for tea in Masham, we think, and when the weather's good enough, you can sit at the table in front of the tea room to watch the people of Masham going about their daily business.

8 Market Place, Masham HG4 4EB
Tel: 01765 688 161
www.fancythattearooms.co.uk

Opening hours

9.30am – 4.00pm Monday – Wednesday
& Friday – Sunday
Closed on Thursdays

MIDDLEHAM

They say Richard III learnt how to make love and war here. He certainly met his wife and spent some time during his formative years at the Castle. Middleham feels such a connection to the guy that they hold an annual requiem mass on the anniversary of his death.

There are 850 human inhabitants of Middleham and over 500 horses, most of the latter being in training. This is one of the country's big horse-race stabling towns and if you time your visit right, you'll see the horses on their way to or from the gallops just outside town.

Twinned with Agincourt in France, though no major battles near Middleham, I don't think!

Tea?

Castle Keep Tea Rooms

The shame about this place is that by the time they open nearly all the race horses have gone back to their stables (or gone racing!) so you won't see many of these beautiful beasts canter past even if you sit out the front and watch. It's a beautiful little tea room, though, backing on to the castle where Richard III spent part of his childhood, and looking out over the cobbled streets of a town which today focuses more on horse-racing than jousting or war. There's a nice selection of home-baked cakes here. Their ginger cake was especially tasty and comes highly recommended. Tea is just Twinings bags, but for a small tea room in a small town/village, they make a nice brew.

Castlehill, Middleham DL8 4QR
Tel: 01969 623 665
http://www.middlehamonline.com/castle_keep.htm

Opening hours

12 noon to 6.00pm Daily (summer hours)
12 noon to 4.00pm Daily (winter hours)
Occasionally open in the mornings in summer

MIDDLESBROUGH

The 100 year-old Transporter Bridge is the town's biggest landmark (260m long and nearly 70m high – visits still possible about once a month). Otherwise, if you like industrial landscapes, this is the town for you! This was the iron and steel capital of the world for many decades. It provided the iron for the Sydney Harbour Bridge and Newcastle's Tyne Bridge. It was so important to British industry that it became the Luftwaffe's first target for bombing in 1940. When the town was first developing in the early-mid 1800s, Prime Minister William Gladstone called it an 'infant Hercules' in English enterprise.

The Council today is making Herculean efforts to regenerate the place, with a new modern art museum called MIMA. Top spot in modern Middlesbrough.

Coffee?

Bahia Cappuccino Bar & Bistro

Owner Eduardo de Melo serves up probably the best cup of coffee you'll get in Middlesbrough; and certainly in the nicest atmosphere. With his background living in Mozambique, South Africa and Brazil, Eduardo knew how to bring an international feel to Middlesbrough, the perfect complement to his wife Joanne, who's a local lass. There's global music playing here all day and as their website says, you can "stay for 10 minutes or all afternoon and enjoy global sounds." Try one of the Italian-style pastries to go with your coffee (three types: chocolate, cappuccino and vanilla cream). This place specialises more on its savoury food, though; after all it is a bistro as well as a cappuccino bar!

300 Linthorpe Road, Middlesbrough TS1 3QU
Tel: 01642 240026
www.bahiabistro.co.uk

Opening hours

8.30am – 5.00pm Monday
8.30am – 9.30pm Tuesday – Saturday
Closed Sundays

Olde Young Tea House

60 types of loose leaf tea to choose from, stored in jars up against the wall as you enter. They encourage you to sniff a few before you choose, but if you can't make up your mind, there's a daily special on offer. Tea comes already steeped so the pot has no leaves in it; if you have a particular way you like your tea, best ask for it! There are home-made cakes, scones for afternoon tea (served on a tiered dish, very elegant) and everything is either made in-house or brought in from local suppliers. Carli Jayne McNaught was just 23 when she opened this tea house in 2010. A fashion enterprise graduate from nearby Saltburn, she has translated her good taste to the world of tea rooms, offering a mix of the olde worlde with the youthful and modern. There are lots of old advertising boards on the walls, alongside the china tea pots. But Carli's very active on social media and posts her daily cake on Facebook most mornings.

84 Grange Road, Middlesbrough TS1 2LS
Tel: 07868 251 420
www.theoldeyoungteahouse.com
Facebook: The Olde Young Tea House
@OldeYoungTHouse

Opening hours

10.00am – 5.00pm Monday – Saturday
Closed Sundays, except for special events

MUKER

The fantastic scenery in this Upper Swaledale village makes the area popular with walkers and cyclists. Oh, and it's on the Tour de France route in 2014, so lots of local cyclists are giving it a go too!

We're not sure why the Muker Silver Band is not a Brass Band, but whatever its metal, its fame has spread through the Dales, a far cry from the local farmers who set the band up in the 1890s.

The village name is pronounced like 'mucus' without the s; definitely not like 'muckier' without the i!

Coffee or tea?

Muker Tea Shop

The tea room is housed in the former village vicarage. The front room is a 'modern' 1890s addition; the really old bits go back to the 1600s. And the setting is quite stunning. Sit out the front for great views over the Dales. It's not often you find coffee of the quality of Grumpy Mule in such an isolated spot, so make the most of it. Tea is all in bags, but good quality too, coming from Taylors of Harrogate. The cakes are home-baked and really are delicious. Top tips: the Old Peculier Fruit Cake, and if they're in season, the plum and almond cake. You can also get a Cream Tea (2 scones and coffee or tea) for just over a fiver.

The Village Stores, Muker, North Yorkshire
DL11 6QG
Tel: 01748 886 409
http://www.mukervillage.co.uk/

Opening hours

Summer opening

10.30am – 5.00pm Monday + Wednesday – Sunday (opening times may vary with weather and demand) Closed Tuesdays

Winter opening

Weekends only

NORTHALLERTON

One of the nicest buildings in town is the Porch House B&B, which Charles I is said to have visited first in 1640 as a guest and later in 1647 as a prisoner. What the blue plaque doesn't add is that the beautiful railings out the front were apparently installed to keep the thousands of cattle heading into town each week out of the front garden space.

The Fleece is said to be the oldest house in town, though, and it was there that Dickens apparently spent a night on one trip up to Yorkshire.

Take a close look at the welcome signs as you drive into town. The capital 'N' was reinstated in 2013 after a vociferous local letter-writing campaign against the decision at first to welcome drivers to 'northallerton'…

Coffee?

Olivia's Artisan Bakery & Café

They use a small, local coffee roaster at Olivia's. Railtown Coffee is Darlington-based and makes a good brew. The baking is pretty special, too. The tray bakes are made by the army veterans bakery in Catterick. But all their bread, scones and some pastries come from the Clervaux Bakery in Darlington, using lots of produce from the eco-farm run by the Clervaux Trust in nearby Croft-on-Tees. The Clervaux Trust started out as a charity running an eco-farm where disadvantaged teenagers could learn all about growing produce sustainably. They then extended the skills-base to introduce baking and show the kids how things go from farm to fork, by opening a café in Darlington. Olivia's is now part of a small social enterprise chain, developing within a 20-mile radius of the original farm and bakery.

127 High Street, Northallerton DL7 8PQ
Tel: 01609 777 377
www.clervauxbakeryandcafe.co.uk
@clervauxcafe

Wifi available

Opening hours

8.00am – 5.00pm Monday – Saturday
10.00am – 4.00pm Sunday

More coffee?

Joe Cornish Gallery Café

A lovely independent coffee shop in this beautiful gallery in Northallerton's old Registry (built 1736). They serve coffee from a new local micro-roaster called Rounton Coffee. It's good stuff, and if you really like it, you might want to attend one of the occasional coffee workshops run here by Rounton. Some of the cakes are baked on-site (recommendation: their moist chocolate & guinness cake), but there are also some things baked at the Angel's Share in nearby Richmond. This place only opened in May 2013 but has already become a hit with locals who know quality when they see it. You're surrounded by Joe Cornish's delightful photos, or work by other artists. And they like their café customers to get their creative juices going, often encouraging draw-it-yourself sessions.

Register House, Zetland Street, Northallerton
DL6 1NA
Tel: 01609 777 404
www.joecornishgallery.co.uk

Opening hours

9.00am – 4.00pm Monday – Saturday
Closed Sundays

Tea?

Bettys Café Tea Rooms

Tea at Bettys is all about Taylors of Harrogate. These are the makers of Yorkshire Tea, but if you're treating yourself to Bettys, why not try something a bit special, like a pot of their loose leaf Assam or Darjeeling. For a cake with your cuppa, the house speciality is surely a Fat Rascal (It's a bit like a cross between a scone and rock cake; delicious with lashings of butter).

Bettys in Northallerton opened 40 years ago and has twice won the Tea Guild's Top Tea award: in 1987 and in 2012. Some members of staff have been around for both awards; that's over 25 years of loyal service. This is our favourite branch of Yorkshire's most famous tea rooms, partly because it has a more intimate feel than the bigger York and Harrogate branches, and partly also because it has a separate 'café' area if you really haven't time for the full afternoon tea experience. But if you do want the works, and those elegant tiered platters, they also have a proper tea room, with waitress service at the back of this very elegant building (it was originally a private residence, with fireplaces even in the toilets, but more recently was Northallerton's branch of a high street bank!).

High Street, Northallerton DL7 8LF
Tel: 01609 775 154
http://www.bettys.co.uk/bettys_northallerton.aspx

Opening hours

9.00am – 5.30pm Monday – Saturday
10.00am – 5.30pm Sunday

OSMOTHERLEY

The start of the Lyke Wake Walk across the North York Moors is about a mile north of Osmotherley. Complete the whole walk across to Ravenscar and you're entitled to have the black coffin badge, a symbol of this path across the Moors used in the past by coffin bearers.

The village itself is a beautifully conserved place, with lovely stone cottages lining the streets. Walk down to the YHA – housed in one of the former flax mills here – and watch the waters cascading over the stepped falls.

Apparently national media turned up during the last Royal wedding because it has the only village pub in the country named the Queen Catherine!

Coffee?

Osmotherley Coffee Shop

This beautiful little village shop used to be the local Post Office, and you'll still find the letter box and red phone booth out the front, a reminder of the days when the GPO did all that kind of thing. It's now a very cosy coffee shop, perfectly-placed for those about to embark on the Lyke Wake Walk, up the road, or in the middle of a Coast-to-Coast trek. The coffee is made with beans roasted by Caffe Society, and if tea takes your fancy, you can get a pot of Yorkshire Tea too. The cakes are all baked either in-house or locally. Top recommendation, if they have any, is their delicious spiced pumpkin and walnut bread or the stem ginger sponge. There's always a good choice, anyway, and there are scones or winter warmers like teacakes and crumpets if you've come in from a walk. There's a beautiful tiled fireplace in the main seating area – decorative now, but another reminder of a bygone age.

West End, Osmotherley DL6 3AA
Tel: 01609 883 818
www.osmotherleywalkingshop.co.uk

Opening hours

Closed Mondays (except Bank Holidays), Tuesdays. Also closed Wednesdays in winter.
10.00am – 4.00pm Thursday – Sunday (+ Wednesday in summer)

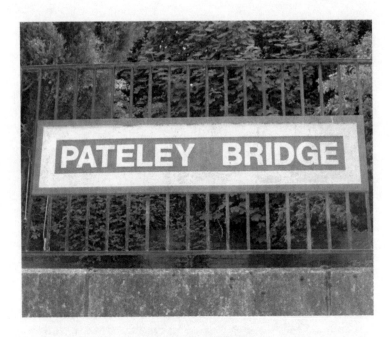

PATELEY BRIDGE

It's hard to imagine this was once a bustling industrial town, with two railways, lead mines, a workhouse and various flax and flour mills. There's more activity now from cyclists hurtling down one of the steep hills into the town...

Fantastic setting along the River Nidd, with views up to the high Dales all around. There's a bandstand with concerts 10 times a year; you can see the old station platforms; and the old workhouse has been converted to a local history museum and arts workshops.

The Oldest Sweet Shop in the World – it opened in 1827 – is right on the High Street, and after featuring on lots of national media, is always a popular stop-off for visitors to Pateley.

The Old Granary Teashop

September 2013 marked the 9th anniversary of Ann, John and Beverley opening up this tea shop in Pateley Bridge's High Street. Ann is yet another who has shifted from teaching to tea, and she now gets her hands in the scone mix every day, with tremendous results. In fact, previous customers have said of their scones: 'best in Yorkshire' and 'best scones in the world...ever', so we had to go in and try. The *Fancy a Cuppa?* team are not into league tables, but we can confirm they are pretty good. And they go down very nicely with a pot of Yorkshire Tea. House speciality is the cheese scone, served with Wensleydale cheese and red onion marmalade. There's also a Nidderdale Cream Tea, at a very reasonable fiver for a scone, cake and pot of tea.

This is an 18th century building, a retail outlet for many years; there's even an old pulley system still in place out the back from the days when big sacks of grain needed to be lifted onto and off the delivery carriages.

17 High Street, Pateley Bridge HG3 5AP
Tel: 01423 711 852
www.oldgranary.net

Opening hours

9.30am – 4.30pm Monday – Wednesday
Closed Thursdays
9.30am – 4.30pm Friday
9.30am – 5.00pm Saturday – Sunday

PICKERING

Pickering's a popular spot just on the edge of the North York Moors. It's at the southern end of the North York Moors Railway, which runs all year round and has lots of steam for railway enthusiasts. There's even an annual 1940s weekend in October and other themed weekends through the year.

Pickering Castle was built to defend against Danes and Scots and its walls survived not only northern invaders but the turmoil of the Civil War and Wars of the Roses. It still towers over the river and railway today.

Coffee?

Café Cocoa

You can tell a coffee shop takes its coffee seriously when the temperature is marked on the menu. If you like your coffee warmer than 60 degrees, you'd better tell them. But I'd much rather have this warning than the other extreme, which is a scalding hot coffee you get in many small town coffee shops. Coffee is excellent here, from Coopers. They also have loose leaf teas, from Taylors of Harrogate. And of course they have patisseries…If it weren't for the cheese scones and Yorkshire curd tart, this window display could be a carbon copy of the finest patisseries of Paris.

A couple of hundred years ago, this must have been a little shop across the road from the local cattle market. There's now a green on that market place where you can take your drink on nice days in summer. Upstairs is the main seating area, with cosy tiffany lamps and lovely local art on the walls. Downstairs are a couple of seats for those unable to climb the stairs and a glorious gallery of the pastries on offer, all made by owner Louise. Her partner Ian runs the chocolate shop just up the road, so you can also sample some of his creations too if you fancy a choc with your cuppa.

6 Smiddy Hill, Pickering YO18 7AN
Tel: 07791 426 843
http://www.cafecocoapatisserie.co.uk/

Opening hours

10.00am – 5.00pm Monday
Closed Tuesdays

Tea?

We suggest a walk or drive to the next village, Middleton, which is just a mile out of Pickering

The Tea Parlour

Owner Dini used to serve afternoon tea in her local village nearby on its annual open gardens day. Locals loved her collection of vintage tea sets and would often urge her to open a tea room of her own. So when the chance came to run the village Post Office in Middleton (that's her son's job now), she spotted an opening for her tea parlour dream. It's all decked out in vintage décor, there'll be 1920s (up to 40s) music playing, and it's got a lovely cosy feel, with a beautiful tiled fireplace in one wall, and everything is served from silver pots into vintage bone china.

Excellent quality loose leaf tea from Taylors of Harrogate, all beautifully-presented. They also have a few special teas, like the wonderful flowering tea, which blooms right in front of your eyes (they get these supplied direct from China). Afternoon tea looks amazing, with sandwiches, scones, jam and cream and then a selection of their home-baked cakes for £9.25 a head (2013 prices).

Main Street, Middleton, Pickering YO18 8NX
Tel: 01751 475 932
www.middletonteaparlour.co.uk

Opening hours

11.00am – 5.00pm Monday (March to October only –
closed Mondays in winter)
Closed Tuesdays
11.00am – 5.00pm Wednesday – Sunday

In Pickering itself...

If it has to be Pickering itself, your best bet is Botham's
of Whitby opposite Pickering station (see our review
under Whitby).

REDCAR

Where the wonderful old Regent Cinema stands now – right on the beach – used to be Redcar's old pier, but it was damaged so often by ships crashing in storms that they gave up on it (the cinema is all that remains).

When they redeveloped the sea front – with lots of new sea defences – they decided to build a 'vertical' pier, which was quickly renamed Redcar Beacon after protests from locals. The Beacon houses our top tip for coffee and tea in Redcar, so we're not complaining.

They filmed part of the WW2 film *Atonement* on Redcar beach. There's a sculpture of a rifle and suitcases next to filing cabinets which presumably is there for film-set lovers. They must have positioned their cameras carefully to miss the wind farm out to sea and the Blade Runneresque scenes of smoking industry just up the beach…We love all those contrasts!

Coffee or tea?

Seasons Restaurant Café

You're right on the sea front here, protected from the waves by a sturdy sea wall, but I'm told that in winter storms the waves can crash over onto the sun terrace – they stay open anyway! Sit here and watch the wind farm or the ships going past on the horizon, and for a closer look, there's a pair of binoculars for customers.

They do the wonderful loose leaf Suki Teas here; we love the Early Grey Blue Flowers any day – a real treat for the taste buds. The coffee is a decent brew – roasted by Tudor in Essex – and the best we could find in Redcar. The cakes are delightful:- all baked on-site at their Richmond café (also reviewed here); top recommendation, if they have any: the lemon poppy seed or the ginger loaf (moist with lovely fresh ginger chunks).

This place started life with the Beacon itself in spring 2013. It's the third in the Seasons family after the Richmond Station venue and one in Darlington. We wouldn't normally review two venues in the same 'chain' but in Redcar we make an exception because of the quality and the views.

Redcar Beacon, Esplanade, Redcar TS10 3AA
Tel: 01642 296 537
www.restaurant-seasons.co.uk

Opening hours

9.00am – 7.00pm Daily

REETH

This was once a centre for lead mining and hand-knitted stockings! There are more remains of the former still visible in the scars on the landscape than there are any sign of stockings!

These days you're more likely to find crowds of fell-walkers or cyclists (especially with the Tour de France passing right through the town in 2014).

It's got more of a village feel now, with a vast green space that allows views around 360 degrees across the Yorkshire Dales landscape. There's no longer a weekly market, but pick the right day in summer and you might find a silver band playing on what's left of the bandstand!

Coffee?

At the time of going to print, there was nowhere in Reeth that stood out for its quality coffee, but there are rumours of a new place due to open in 2014, so by the time this book is published, it may well be there. Ask a local!

Tea?

Ivy Cottage Tea Room / B&B

A steaming pot of Yorkshire Tea awaits when you sit down for tea in this lovely tea room right on Reeth's green (tea bags only, but so much else here compensates for that!). The home baking is fabulous. Owner Mike is a dab hand at baking bread, tea cakes and scones. And there's usually a cake or two on offer, also baked in-house of course.

Janet and Mike have been running this B&B and tea room for about eight years now and, if the warm welcome and chatty approach is anything to go by, they love it as much today as they did at the beginning. One American visitor liked it so much, he sent them a framed sketch of the place after he returned home to the States – it hangs on the wall alongside the tea and coffee adverts and Dales photos.

Reeth Green, Reeth DL11 6SF
Tel 01748 884 418
www.ivycottagereeth.co.uk

Opening hours

Vary with the seasons so phone to check
12noon – 5.00pm Monday
Closed Tuesdays
12noon – 5.00pm Wednesday – Sunday
(tend to open an hour earlier in winter – when fewer
B&B guests to serve in the morning!)

RICHMOND

This is still one of the prettiest market towns in North Yorkshire, but imagine how it must have looked when its Georgian Theatre was first built (1788) and there was horse racing up on the very top of the hill above town (the remains of the Georgian grandstand are still there – with great views all around).

The Castle still dominates the skyline here; take the Castle Walk for views down over the River Swale and onto the grassy area that once hosted jousting matches, but now has the local football club on its turf.

Legend has it that there are tunnels all over (or under) the town, many leading to and from the Castle and nearby Easby Abbey. One story tells that a drummer boy disappeared down one tunnel, and a stone still stands on the spot where his drumming was last heard. Locals know where the tunnel entrance is, apparently, but we couldn't possibly tell you…Far too dangerous!

Coffee?

Sip Coffee

This is a classic cosy coffee shop just a few yards from the Market Place. It's the best venue in Richmond for a sit-down-and-feel-at-home-for-a-while cuppa. Coffee is from Caffe Society down near York which makes a good strong, but smooth cappuccino. There's also a good selection of tray bakes – flapjacks (made by owner Andy); and usually a sponge cake (made by Andy's wife).

I won't tell you where owner Andy comes from, but the football up on the shelf behind the bar might give you a clue. Oh, and check out the map of the world: he's marked most of the other Richmonds wherever they are across the globe.

18 King Street, Richmond DL10 4HP
Tel: 01748 822 877
Facebook: Sip Coffee

Wifi available
No toilets here – nearest in the indoor market or the Nuns Close car park

Opening hours

9.15am – 4.00pm Monday – Friday
9.00am – 4.00pm Saturday
10.00am – 4.00pm Sunday

More coffee?

Mocha

The only place in town you can get Grumpy Mule coffee. And these guys take great pride in their product. With chocolates their forte, you'll always be offered a choc with your cup, and they do try lots of drink specials, often with a chocolate theme to them. It's takeaway only (for now anyway), but they have a bench outside to sit and watch the world go by.

Elizabeth and Dennis are relative newcomers to North Yorkshire, having moved up from Lincolnshire in the summer of 2013 to start this new venture. But they have quickly established themselves in this market town community and are the first to dress their shop window for local festivities, be it the Walking and Book Festival, Halloween or Christmas.

1 Trinity Church Square, Richmond DL10 4HY
Tel: 07950 211 218
www.mochachocolateshop.co.uk

No toilets here – nearest in the indoor market

Opening hours

9.30am – 5.00pm Monday – Tuesday
Closed Wednesdays
9.30am – 5.00pm Thursday – Saturday
11.00am – 5.00pm Sunday

Seasons Café

This is the place to come in Richmond for a pot of loose leaf tea. It's the excellent Suki Tea so it's worth coming down here from the centre of town for a cuppa of this quality. Cakes are all baked in-house (and actually delivered from here to the branch in Redcar that we also review here). But it's the setting that makes this place special (as well as the tea). This is Richmond's old railway station, converted some years ago to a community hub, with cinema, independent shops and this rather nice café/restaurant. You might even be sitting on an old platform or by the old tracks, and if you're interested in the days when this was a working station, there is a permanent exhibition in one of the old waiting rooms showing film footage of the days when it was normal to catch a train from Richmond to Darlington!

Richmond Station, DL10 4LD
Tel: 01748 825 340
www.restaurant-seasons.co.uk

Opening hours

9.00am – 9.00pm Monday – Thursday
9.00am – 10.00pm Friday – Saturday
9.00am – 7.00pm Sunday

RIPON

Ripon once aspired to being a spa town. It was always too close to Harrogate to compete, but we love its 1904 swimming baths, which still stand today. 100 years ago, you could get an Aixe Douche & Massage for 3/6 (17.5p in new money); a D'Arsonval Current 10 minutes for 2/6; and a 2nd class salt bath for 1/6. The building is as dramatic outside today as it was in 1905, and some of the original fittings are still in the pool itself!

There used to be a 9pm curfew here, and the Wakeman was in charge through the night to keep the peace. He still blows his horn at 9pm every evening and his image (or his horn) is dotted all over town, though I'm not sure how much time he spends dealing with late-night revellers these days…

Ripon Cathedral's a great spot for looking up Lewis Carroll stories, seeing George Washington's arms and finding the hole women used to have to squeeze through to prove their chastity! It's also a very beautiful building.

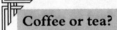

Coffee or tea?

Oliver's Pantry

Tim and Louise opened Oliver's Pantry in July 2012, taking on a retail space that had lain empty for about 30 years and transforming it into a thriving coffee shop. They have a board outside claiming the 'best coffee in Ripon', and we have to agree. They use Grumpy Mule beans, roasted just down the road in Yorkshire. They're also proud of their loose leaf teas, which come from Jeeves & Jericho in Oxford. And the cakes are all either baked in-house or made locally by small independent bakers.

This used to be a ginger beer bottling plant, and they've not only kept some old ginger beer bottles for display, but they have some of the machinery on view out the back, where you can sit in summer. Their sympathetic refurbishment led to a framed recognition from the local historical society, displayed on the walls of the coffee shop.

86 North Street, Ripon HG4 1DP
Tel: 01765 600 548
http://www.oliverspantry.com/
@oliverspantry

Opening hours

8.30am – 5.00pm Monday – Saturday
10.00am – 4.00pm Sunday

ROBIN HOOD'S BAY

There's nothing to prove Robin Hood ever came anywhere near this place, but don't let that put you off visiting. It's a wonderful old village full of cobbled streets and narrow lanes right down a steep hill.

It must have been a perfect place for a spot of smuggling, and that happened quite a bit in the late 1700s, including lots of tea smuggled in mostly from Holland, which had Far East connections as good as ours were in those days.

One of the most extraordinary stories in its history, though, came when a ship ran aground in a storm in 1881. Conditions were so treacherous, they had to bring the lifeboat in from Whitby, but over land, through snowdrifts and down the steep slope to the village. And look out for the photo in one shop window of the day in the 1950s when a bus got stuck on the bend in the road. You'll see why it's best to walk down here!

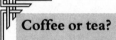

Coffee or tea?

Swell Café Bar

The café website has extraordinary photos of when this 18th century Wesleyan Chapel was derelict in the 1980s. It had closed as a chapel when coastal erosion threatened it from behind in the 1930s, but now Swell Café has a protective coastal walkway running just below the café terrace. You get a bit of sea spray in a storm but on a fine day, this must surely be one of the finest views around. And if you really fall in love with this place, it's also possible to hire it as a wedding venue!

Coffee and tea here supplied by that old family firm Ringtons. You won't find a better cuppa anywhere in Robin Hood's Bay, nor with better views than this! Their scones and toasted teacakes go down nicely with a brew on a blustery day.

The Old Chapel, Chapel Street, Robin Hood's Bay YO22 4SQ
Tel: 01947 880 180
www.swellcafe.co.uk

Opening hours

10.00am – 3.00pm Daily

SALTBURN

There wasn't a single pub in Saltburn when the town was first built, because it was established by the tee-total Quaker Pease family; can't imagine the smugglers down on the beach had the same attitude, mind (shame the old smugglers museum is now closed).

The cliff lift (still water-powered to this day) is one of the town's highlights; it takes you down to the pier, which is regularly 'yarn-bombed', drawing crowds in to see what Saltburn's mystery knitters have been doing recently.

At low tide, you can really imagine Malcolm Campbell in Blue Bird achieving the land speed record in 1922 – Shame we found nothing to mark that event.

The Vista Mar bistro was once an elegant tea room looking out over the beach; just above there is a house known as 'Teddy's Nook' because it is allegedly where Edward VII used to meet Lillie Langtry before he came to the throne.

The Sitting Room

Becky and Bob are two local artists who have their studio on the premises, but use the space downstairs for this rather special tea room in what was, presumably, a Saltburn station waiting room. They also run the artwork and antique shop next door. There's a lovely old fireplace on one side, lots of photographs on display and shelves filled with a mix of tea pots, tea cups and…vintage cameras. A stylish venue in a great spot.

There's a wonderful selection of loose leaf teas here, supplied by Leaf Shop in London. We chose an uplifting tea from Nepal called 'Roof of the World', but there was also a quality Kenyan, Darjeeling, Earl Grey and some interesting variations like black tea with rose petals and black tea with lychee. The cakes are pretty special, too. Baked by a lady living in nearby Redcar, the house speciality is a white chocolate pistachio sponge. And great service from Sam and Christine who'll give you a warm welcome.

3-4 Station Buildings, Saltburn-by-the-Sea TS12 1AQ
Tel: 01287 626 150
Facebook: Profile Gallery & The Sitting Room

Opening hours

10.00am – 4.00pm Monday
Closed Tuesdays and Wednesdays
10.00am – 4.00pm Thursday – Friday
10.00am – 5.00pm Saturday
10.00am – 4.00pm Sunday

Coffee?

Camfields Espresso Bar

Boyd Camfield and his brother turned this old ticket office from Saltburn's miniature railway into a coffee shop with great views over to the beach. The perfect spot to sit in the sun and watch the tide come in. But, don't worry, they close the windows if it rains, so you can sit inside; and when it's a bit chilly with that sea breeze blowing, you can huddle up out the back on the terrace and shelter from the storm.

The Illy Espresso on offer at Camfields is a cut above the coffee you can get anywhere else we found in Saltburn. There's nowhere to bake on the premises, so you can't expect cakes made in-house, but the scones and traybakes are made locally and went down very nicely, thank you.

Valley Gardens, Saltburn-by-the-Sea TS12 1NY
Tel: 01287 626 070
www.camfields.co.uk
Facebook: Camfields Espresso Bar

Wifi available
No toilets here – nearest are by the car park 200 metres away

Opening hours

9.00am – 5.00pm Daily (summer)
9.00am – 4.00pm Daily (winter)

More Tea and a walk – or mini train ride?

Valley Gardens Tea Room

This tea room is tucked away at the back of Saltburn's lovely Valley Gardens, built by the Pease family in the 19th century. There are the beautiful Italian Gardens next door, and a whole lawn in front of the tea room, so it's ideal for dog walkers and for families with kids who want a safe place to play. Owner Lorna bakes a mean cake; she gets most of the ideas from a vintage recipe book she has, and they are fantastic. We opted for a Victoria Sandwich Cake, but I'm told the various fruit cake recipes are most popular. Beautifully presented with a pot of cream and a strawberry. And they all wash down easily with a big pot of Yorkshire Tea.

If you're on the Cleveland Way, it's only a small detour; and if you can't face the walk here from the beach (it's a good half mile), you can catch the miniature railway. Or get here down the path from the Bandstand in the town centre.

Valley Gardens, Saltburn-by-the-Sea TS12 1JS
Tel: 01287 626 792
http://www.thevalleygardenstearooms.co.uk/

Opening hours

July-September – Opens daily at 10.00am
May-June – Tuesday-Sunday Opens at 10.00am
March-April + October – Wednesday – Sunday – Opens at 10.00am
December-January-February – redecoration and

maintenance time, though they may open on occasional days.

Closes around 5.00pm, but can be later if busy in summer, and earlier if wet and quiet.

SCARBOROUGH

The Scarborough Fair – the one where you could buy 'parsley, sage, rosemary and thyme' – ran from 1253 till the 18th century. Scarborough was already a spa town in the 1660s, when wealthier folk could come for their health and a holiday.

It was the coming of the railway in the 1800s that made this into a more popular holiday resort. The train station even today lays claim to having the world's longest seat (on Platform 1), though some say it used to stretch almost as far as Seamer.

Anne Bronte died in Scarborough in 1849 and is buried up near the Castle, at St Mary's Church. There's a blue plaque on the side of the Grand Hotel, though she wasn't staying there; the hotel was built a few years after her passing.

The Grand is perhaps Scarborough's most majestic feature.

With its 4 towers, 12 floors, 52 chimneys and 365 rooms, you certainly get the feeling its architect or owner had a thing about time. And I'm sure he (surely a 'he') would be delighted that it still dominates the south beach almost 150 years on.

Alan Aykbourn premiered 75 of his plays in Scarborough, many of them at the Stephen Joseph Theatre, which is now in the wonderful 1930s former Odeon Cinema building opposite the station – AND they still show films there, too!

Coffee?

Roasters Coffee Company

It's rare to find coffee so far north from Peter James, the excellent roasters in Ross-on-Wye. They do a blend just for Roasters in Scarborough. There's a nice range of scones, all baked locally, to go with your coffee. Best coffee in Scarborough? Surely!

Alex Buckley is a local lad who used to work here when he was still at school. He jumped at the chance to take on the place when it became available in March 2013. Some might say it's a tough act to follow, since this coffee shop used to be run by three-times UK Barista Champion Simon Robertson. But he's going about things the right way, keeping great suppliers like Peter James. And he has a good loyal customer base, including a few from the cast of Coronation Street, so keep your eyes peeled if you seek celebrity!

8 Aberdeen Walk, Scarborough YO11 1XP
Tel: 01723 361 922
www.roasterscoffee.co.uk

Opening hours

8.00am – 5.30pm Monday – Saturday
9.30am – 4.00pm Sunday

Tea?

Francis Tea Room

What a wonderful tea room. First of all, there's the great choice of 16 loose leaf teas. Then there's the fantastic Afternoon Tea beautifully-presented on tiered platters, with delicious delicate sandwiches, slices of home-baked cake and a mini scone with cream and jam for those who like a Cream Tea but want a bit more... And then the extraordinary venue itself, which started life as Ced Francis' ladies' hair salon in the 1940s (one of the tea room's current regulars remembers coming here for a styling in 1949!).

Privacy was clearly important to ladies in curlers and hairdryers because the old salon cubicles are still in place; only now it means you can sip your pot of Darjeeling in private instead. The old hairdresser's name is still engraved on the door window, so when Brad and Sarah took this tea room on in August 2012, they renamed it Francis Tea Rooms. These two are a great example of people who lose their jobs in completely different professions, but turn that into an opportunity by opening a tearoom like this. It's a long way from Brighton, where they used to live, but some call Scarborough the 'Brighton of the North', so you can see why they chose to move here...

7 South Street, Scarborough YO11 2BP
Tel: 01723 350 550
http://francistearooms.wix.com/home

Opening hours

Closed Mondays
10.30am – 4.00pm Tuesday – Saturday
11.00am – 3.30pm Sunday (May – October)

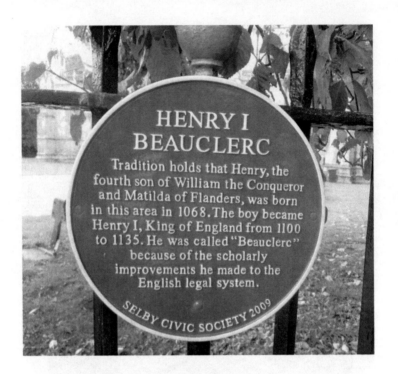

SELBY

The first railway station ever to be built in Yorkshire was in Selby. The building still exists, but is a warehouse now, some way from the current station on the East Coast mainline.

In those days, it was a 6-hour ride by paddle steamer to get here from Hull, and the story goes that Johann Strauss brought his orchestra from Europe that way, then walked along the High Street with the musicians to catch a train from Selby!

Going back further, it is said that William the Conqueror's son, Henry I, was born in Selby. And the Abbey has a stained-glass window bearing the Washington family arms, which became the blueprint for the Stars and Stripes.

The Rainbow Warrior ship blown up by French marines in New Zealand was launched (under a different name) in Selby in 1957. The old shipyard is now derelict, with no reminder left of this or other famous vessels that started life here.

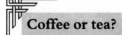

Coffee or tea?

Hope Yard Café

This café in one of Selby's oldest streets is a hit with local cyclists who need a pitstop on a ride through Yorkshire. A nice cup of coffee (beans from Grand Milano) and a bacon sandwich set the cyclists back on the road. And if you time it right, you might also get a piece of home-baked cake, with a gluten-free option also usually available. Since our visit, they've started using the wonderful Eteaket teas – loose leaf, from the award-winning suppliers in Edinburgh – so we'll be back for tea soon!

Lovely photos all over the walls here show the times when this establishment was a fruit and flower shop, also selling fish and game! How different times were then. Gillian, who runs the place these days, abandoned her career in IT to set up this coffee shop; she and partner Martin are keen cyclists themselves, so this place is popular with local pedallers – and they're happy to fill your water bottle too before you get back on the saddle. A friendly vibe in the heart of Selby.

49 Micklegate, Selby YO8 4EA
Tel: 07904 461 176
Facebook: HopeYardCafe

Opening hours

8.30am – 3.30pm Monday – Friday
8.30am – 3.15pm Saturday
Closed Sundays

More coffee?

Osteria 23

The friendly family who run this place are NOT Italian. No, they are from Sardinia and proud of it! They moved to the Selby area four years ago after spotting a gap in the market locally for good food and coffee. Arianna runs the deli and coffee shop and other family members have the 'Italian' restaurant round the corner in Millgate. Having said that, Osteria23 is the nearest you'll get in this part of Yorkshire to a genuine Italian coffee experience. They use Caffe Vergnano 1882: Italian, but roasted in London. Their specialities on the pastry side of things are also imported direct from Italy. And if you sit out on the terrace on a fine day, you can ALMOST imagine you're in Italy (or Sardinia) rather than Selby…

Unit 10, Market Cross Shopping Centre,
Selby YO8 4JS
Tel: 07588 545 098
www.osteria23.co.uk

Opening hours

9.00am – 5.00pm Monday – Saturday
Closed (usually) on Sundays

SETTLE

Best views of town come from Castlebergh Rock. It's a tough five minute walk from the Market Place via Constitution Hill. In earlier days, this was a bit of a pleasure park, with swings and roundabouts half way up, and a gatekeeper who'd offer boiling water to make your tea for the picnic up there.

Settle railway station is full of memorabilia for train enthusiasts. This is of course the start of the Settle-Carlisle Railway, and there are old signals, signal box, water tower and photos of the line in days gone by. Views from here are pretty good, too!

Take a look at the Telephone Box Gallery. It's on The Green, in an old red phone box, and it exhibits work by local artists. Nice community touch.

Coffee?

The Kitchen Café

There's a real sense of community to this coffee shop upstairs above an interiors and kitchenware shop on Settle's Market Place. Owner Andy has a real passion for what he does, having shifted from his previous career as an investment banker. He says he hasn't witnessed a marriage proposal here yet, but virtually everything else happens here, and there's a very positive vibe. You might find fewer of the visiting tourists here than in some of other venues in the Market Place, but that's probably because it is less immediately visible as you get off the coach!

The Taylors of Harrogate coffee (they have at least four different blends available according to the strength you like) tempted me into choosing a cafetiere rather than a cappuccino (they use a different roast/brand for the espresso machine). Cakes are baked right in front of you in the kitchen; scones, too. Our recommendation: the Ginger & Guinness sponge cake. The freshly-grilled sausages and the soup looked good too, but we just do cake for these reviews…

Market Place, Settle BD24 9EF
Tel: 07717 395 541
Facebook: The Kitchen Cafe

Opening hours

9.00am – 5.30pm Monday – Saturday
10.30am – 5.00pm Sunday

Tea?

Poppies Tea Room

This tea room is tucked away from Settle's main street and market area, but is worth finding. Thomas Croll has been running this place for seven years and he has created the nicest décor of all the town's tea rooms, with stylish colours and local art on the walls. Also an interesting ornate pillar in the middle of the room – apparently it's one of a pair which keeps the building standing, but nobody is quite sure why it's there. Maybe the entrance to the theatre which apparently used to be on this site many moons ago? You'll get a good pot of Birchall Tea here and the cakes are excellent, all home-baked, with a good gluten-free selection.

Bishopdale Court, Settle BD24 9EB
Tel: 07932 182 293
Facebook: Poppies Tea Room

Opening hours

8.30am – 4.30pm Monday – Tuesday
8.30am – 3.00pm Wednesday
8.30am – 4.30pm Thursday – Saturday
10.00am – 4.00pm Sunday

SKIPTON

'Fiery' Fred Trueman has a statue next to Skipton's main car park. He wasn't born here, but he did run a sports shop in town after he retired. Probably had most of his tea at Headingley, mind.

They don't shout it from the rooftops, but during the Wars of the Roses, Skipton actually sided with the Red Rose crowd. Some say that's why their castle stayed so intact. I'm not sure why the French word 'Désormais' is carved in stone above the castle entrance, though.

The Spencer half of Marks & Spencer was born in Skipton. There is a commemorative plaque, but it's quite hard to read (just above head height at the bottom of the High Street).

The 1770s Leeds-Liverpool Canal runs right through town.

Coffee?

Bean Loved

Co-owner Wes was among the UK's top 10 baristas at the UK Barista Championships in 2013. Not surprising, then, that you get a great coffee here, especially when combined with the excellent Grumpy Mule coffee beans and their beautiful mahogany red Marzocco espresso machine. They also have a guest espresso, to give regulars in Skipton a taste of something a bit different sometimes. If it's tea you're after, they have several loose leaf blends put together by the excellent Suki Teas.

This is a father and son business, with Steve (the Dad) leading in the kitchen. Wes went south for his coffee knowledge, working in Australia and New Zealand for a couple of years to fine-tune his barista skills. But he came back to Yorkshire to join his father at Bean Loved, and there's even more family locally, with an uncle running a local garage and his grandparents also Skipton-based.

17 Otley Street, Skipton BD23 1DY
Tel: 01756 791 534
http://www.beanloved.co.uk/
@beanloved

Wifi available

Opening hours

7.30am – 5.00pm Monday – Friday
8.00am – 5.00pm Saturday
9.00am – 5.00pm Sunday

Tea?

The Three Sheep Tearoom

Tracy and Charlotte are a mother/daughter team. The tea room got its name from a nice combination of the local and the personal: the name 'Skipton' comes from 'sheep town' in old English, so sheep had to come into it somewhere; and Tracy used to work in office number 3 when she worked for the local authority before this, so there had to be three sheep!

There's a nice selection of loose leaf teas from Taylors of Harrogate. The cakes and scones are all baked in-house. They have about six cakes on the go at any one time (we spotted: orange & lemon sponge; date & walnut; coffee; paradise slice), and the scones just keep appearing by the dozen (Charlotte reckons she makes 10 dozen a day at the moment!). There's seating upstairs or down, and a few out the front on the pedestrianised side.

78 High Street, Skipton BD23 3LX
Tel: 01756 709988
No web presence

Opening hours

9.30am – 5.00pm Monday
Closed Tuesdays (except during school holidays, when open 7 days a week)
9.30am – 5.00pm Wednesday – Friday
9.00am – 5.00pm Saturday
10.00am – 4.30pm Sunday

135

STAITHES

The shop where Captain Cook got his first job as a teenager was destroyed by a storm surge over a hundred years ago. On the same spot today is a building called Captain Cook's Cottage – protected these days by a new harbour wall and sea defences.

Fishing (along with tourism) makes up a major part of village life even today; and you'll see instructions in the Harbour Office window for the minimum size of fish that can be legally caught, including cod, haddock and bass!

It's a steep hill down to the village. If you can't make it down, there's always our tea room at the top, and take a look at the old World War One army camp, which still operates as holiday 'chalets'.

The Tea Shop

Run by mother/daughter team of Angela and Lou, it's a real family affair this place. Angela's uncle not only provides the fruit from his garden for the cakes, but the veg for the daily soup; her husband grows the lettuce and bakes the odd cake. And being local, Angela's Mum can remember the days when this tea room would even host wedding receptions for local couples: they have a wonderful wedding invitation from February 1952 when guests of Wilf and Cecilia were invited back to The Cabin Tea Shop for tea.

The tea is a standard Yorkshire Tea (bags only), but that's our tea of choice at home so we're always happy to have it out too, especially in lovely surroundings like these. There's a great selection of home-baked cakes, with a blueberry bakewell topping the bill on the day we visited.

The person doing the washing up gets the best views down over the valley, but don't worry: they tend to call guests over if deer wander up to the window...

83 Staithes Lane, Staithes TS13 5AD
No web presence

Opening hours

10.00am – 4.00pm Daily (March – November)
10.00am – 4.00pm Thursday – Sunday (December-February – closed Monday – Wednesday in winter)

Coffee?

Seadrift Café

Lovely spot for a cuppa before (or after) a walk on the beach. Vicky Gale has been in charge of this place for some 7 years now, but it had been in her family for 20 years before that. Must have been an interesting place to have a cuppa in a real gale, before they built the new sea defences. This café is right over the road from the harbour and even today at high tide the waters lap right up to the sea wall in front.

Not surprising it's a good coffee when you find out that it's made by Bollings in Yorkshire, the home of Grumpy Mule Coffee. They also bake all their own cakes, but the house speciality is called a Staithes Coble (pronounced cobble) Cake with apricot, walnut, apple and cinnamon; delicious warmed and served with cream – it's an old family recipe.

Seaton Garth, Staithes TS13 5DH
Tel: 01947 841 345
No web presence

Opening hours

10.00am – 4.00pm Monday – Wednesday
Closed Thursdays and Fridays
10.00am – 4.00pm Saturday – Sunday
(Closed in January – and times might change in winter)

138

STOKESLEY

Stokesley's biggest claim to worldwide fame surely comes via the company that produces Quorn just on the outskirts of town.

Australian visitors tend to head to the centre of Stokesley to spot the yellow painted house right by the river, which was where Jane Pace lived: she was the first white woman to settle in Victoria.

Lots of ways of crossing the River Leven, even today. A narrow 17th century 'pack horse' bridge (not wide enough for carts, though); a ford used mainly by ducks these days; low-level walking 'bridges' that are more slabs of concrete; and the more modern bridge that even takes cars!

Coffee or tea?

Bexter's Tea Room

Best coffee in Stokesley by a long way: Limini Coffee is always good, but they do a special blend just for Bexters (and you can buy a packet of the ground stuff if you like what you drink). The tea is pretty special here, too. It's the first time we'd come across Holmfirth Tea: it's a small West Yorkshire blending company that do delicious loose leaf teas. We had the 'Original' blend, but they do all sorts of loose leaf, including a green tea and a fruit tea. Scones are baked by co-owner Jayne, but most of the other cakes are baked by Linda Martin in nearby Nunthorpe, who works under the name The Cake Shelf. This is a tastefully-built extension to the old school building in town, and if you sit out on the terrace, chances are you'll see the Sunday School entrance carved into the stone below your gaze.

The Church House, 30 College Square,
Stokesley TS9 5DN
Tel: 01642 712 811
@bexterstearoom
Facebook: Bexters Tea Room

Opening hours

9.00am – 5.00pm Monday – Saturday
Closed Sundays

TADCASTER

The smell of malt will likely hit you before you even step outside in Tadcaster. Its three breweries dominate the town; Sam Smith's is the oldest (formed in 1758) and if you're lucky you'll see their horse and cart deliveries trotting up the High Street.

The Town Council occupies the most beautiful building in town, though. The Ark is a classic Tudor manor house, where it is thought that the Pilgrim Fathers met before embarking on their voyage across to America.

The Romans were here a bit earlier, mind you. When the town was called Calcaria (because of the limestone nearby), the River Wharfe was crossed by a ford, though you wouldn't want to try that in a high water flood...

Tea?

The Tea Lounge

They do a nice pot of Yorkshire Tea here, beautifully presented in blue tea pots and the Tea Lounge's own cups and saucers. But it's the cakes that make this place really special. Owner Lisa makes them all herself from recipes passed down from her Granny (she says she'll publish a book of them one day, but for now they're all in her head!). There were scones, lemon cake, chocolate cake, but the specialities of the house are the meringues, and the interesting creation on the day of our visit was a Tea Lounge Slice, consisting of meringue, white chocolate, cranberries and almond – delicious! You can also get a full Afternoon Tea for just over a tenner, with sandwich, scone, cake and a pot of tea.

For many years, this building was a music shop run by a Mr Lovely, who called it 'Lovely Music'! After he retired, Lisa Thompson's husband was employed to do some refurbishing, so was tipped the wink when the place was available for let. He passed the message on to Lisa, who had been baking in the catering trade for years and was dying to run her own tea room. And it's been a great success.

17 Westgate, Tadcaster LS24 9JB
Tel: 01937 831 800
No web presence

Opening hours

9.00am – 4.00pm Monday – Tuesday
Closed Wednesdays

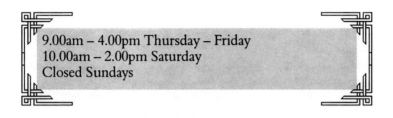

9.00am – 4.00pm Thursday – Friday
10.00am – 2.00pm Saturday
Closed Sundays

Coffee?

The Granary

This is the place to go for coffee in Tadcaster. They use Caffe Society, which does you a nice, smooth cappuccino, and is roasted just down the road from here. The scones are baked fresh every day on-site, and we timed our visit perfectly, just as the latest batch were coming out of the oven.

This building is actually owned by the Sam Smith's Brewery, which has been in town for over 250 years and is just across the road from the café. If you're lucky you'll see the dray horses pulling the Sam Smith's delivery cart past as you sip your coffee. But then you may want to stay for lunch and a bottle of beer with it (yes, they also sell Sam Smith's here!).

28 Bridge Street, Tadcaster LS24 9AL
Tel: 01937 833 529
www.thegranarytadcaster.co.uk
@thegranarytad

Opening hours

Closed Mondays
9.00am – 2.30pm Tuesday – Saturday
(also open for meals 6.00pm – 9.00pm)
12noon – 3.00pm Sunday

THIRSK

Thomas Lord, who went on to lay the turf for English cricket's HQ, was born in Thirsk. There's an outline of two men with mugs of tea (or coffee) in their hands in the upstairs window of his former home, now the town museum. Surely not a reference to tea breaks at test matches?

Thirsk's other famous son is James Herriot, whose former veterinary practice is now the World of James Herriot. The plaque bearing his real name, Alfred Wight, still stands on the door of the building; and he married in the church up the road.

The Ritz Cinema first showed films in 1912 and is one of the few cinemas left from that era where you can still see films today.

Coffee?

Courthouse Café

The nicest cup of coffee we had in Thirsk, roasted by a supplier called Chartley in Stafford – our first time tasting their coffee. Although we chose it for our coffee in Thirsk, the Courthouse cream teas have also been getting more and more popular. The scones, along with the traybakes, flapjacks and brownies are baked by the in-house café team or by a local lady known as The Cake Fairy (real name: Claire Taylor). In a nice addition to the 'menu', they have flapjack recipe cards by Yorkshire-based Busy Flowers, and if you buy one of the flapjacks made to these recipes you get a discount on the cards!

Bex Griffiths became manager of the Courthouse Café in February 2013. After a career in marketing and being a PA, running this business and baking every day is a complete change, one she's clearly thriving on. This was Thirsk's local court from the mid-1800s until 1995. It's now part of the Rural Arts centre, with arts workshops, exhibitions and an arty gift shop.

The Old Courthouse, Westgate, Thirsk YO7 1QS
Tel: 07542 143 943 – 01845 526 536
www.ruralarts.org
@ruralarts

Wifi available

Opening hours

10.00am – 4.30pm Monday – Saturday
Closed Sundays

Upstairs Downstairs Deli

Thierry Boero comes originally from the beautiful town of Besançon in eastern France. But after going to hotel school and working for many years in London's 5-star hotel scene, he came north to Thirsk in 2005 and set up these tea rooms with his wife Bridget. There's nothing aloof or haughty about the 5-star service they are giving to the people of Thirsk. They know their regulars by name and are just as friendly with the strangers who fill the place on market days or race days.

All the teas on the menu – and for sale downstairs in the deli – are from Taylors of Harrogate. You can go for the ever-popular Yorkshire Tea or something a little more special like an Assam or Lapsang. The food is all prepared on-site, with produce bought locally. Top tip: freshly-baked scones or the Yorkshire Curd tarts. Bread comes from Clarks of Easingwold, and that's about as far afield as they go for their food and drink!

25-27 Market Place, Thirsk YO7 1HD
Tel: 01845 526 067
Facebook: Upstairs Downstairs

Opening hours

8.00am – 4.00pm Monday – Saturday
Closed Sundays

THORNTON-LE-DALE

There surely can't be a more picturesque village in North Yorkshire than Thornton-le-Dale. One particular thatched cottage gets itself onto lots of chocolate boxes and biscuit barrels, but really the whole village could, from the alms houses lining the main street to the big, grand Hall opposite.

And there's water everywhere here: streams flow gently through the village (except, I guess, when they deal with storm wash from the Moors), from the car park to the village green.

There's no market here anymore but the old market cross still stands; in summer they have brass band concerts and in winter it's the setting for the Christmas lights...all along those streams!

Lavenders Tea Room

There's a good range of loose leaf teas here from Taylors of Harrogate. The Ceylon, Darjeeling, Assam, Earl Grey or simple English Breakfast are also excellent and there's green tea and rose petal tea for aficionados of such things. A nice touch is the stopwatch to advise you on how long you should let the tea brew; also the hand-knitted tea cosies. There are lots of lovely options for Afternoon Tea: The basic Cream Tea is a pot of Yorkshire Tea with scone, cream and jam; the Savoury Cream Tea gives you a cheese scone instead and some cream cheese for filling, with chutney; or the Afternoon Tea on a tiered platter, with sandwich, home-baked cake and two scones, with the loose leaf tea of your choice.

This 14th century forge is the oldest building in the village. You can sit out the front and watch the stream trickling by or take a seat inside where the décor is tastefully modern, but with a rustic look. There's lots of lavender on display, too. And why 'lavender'? Apparently, the previous owner had a dream of running her own tea rooms for years when she lived in the Middle East and had always decided that would be the name – and the theme – of her tea room.

The Forge, Thornton-le-Dale, YO18 7RN
Tel: 01751 475013
www.lavenders.uk.com

Opening hours

10.00am – 5.00pm Daily
(Closed Mondays from October to March)

WHITBY

Dracula is so much a part of our culture now that it's hard to believe he was only conceived by Bram Stoker some years after our favourite tea room first opened! Those who attend one of Whitby's two Goth Weekends probably don't care that he was in fact another Victorian invention! And Whitby is a great setting for vampire-themed stories…

Up on Whitby's West Cliff are the iconic statue of Captain Cook and the whale bone arch. Whaling out of Whitby was going strong when Cook first went to sea, though he got his sea legs transporting coal up and down the coast.

The street layout can't have changed much for centuries:

narrow cobbled lanes on the east side under the cliff where the Abbey stands (lots of jet workshops; kippers being smoked; and arty gift shops); the sandy beach begins on the west side, with one of those beach lifts built in the 1930s.

Coffee?

Java Café

Nice cup of coffee in a great spot for watching the people of Whitby go by, especially during Whitby's twice-yearly Goth Weekends. Owner Ben, who set this place up ten years ago, has had a colourful life, working many years as a chef, during which time he worked alongside Gordon Ramsay at one point. He now also offers his time as a volunteer lifeboat crew member, so he's very much part of the local community in a town like Whitby. They use Eros Coffee, a fair-trade coffee blend that gives you a pretty smooth cappuccino. Not all cakes are baked in-house, so it's worth asking if that matters to you. I chose the home-baked cheesecake, made by manager Lacey. Delicious!

2a Flowergate, Whitby YO21 3BA
Tel: 01947 821 973
Facebook: Java Cafe Whitby
Wifi available

Opening hours

8.00am – 6.00pm Daily

Botham's of Whitby

Elizabeth Botham began selling cakes at Whitby market to make ends meet in the mid 1860s after the family lost their farm to cattle plague. Her baking was so popular that she opened a shop, and this tea room today is still on the original premises of the first café in the Botham's name. Some of Elizabeth's great grandchildren are still running the business today, and a new generation, the great-great grandchildren, are also getting in on the act now. Who can blame them with such a fabulous tea room and bakery? Nick & Jo supervise the baking (Nick also works shifts for the local lifeboat); Mike takes the lead on tea; Sarah manages the shops; and Liz & Lois decorate the cakes. Details of the others are on the Botham's website. Can't wait for their 150th anniversary in 2015!

There's a fantastic choice of loose leaf teas at Botham's. From their basic English Breakfast (an Assam, Kenya, Ceylon blend) through to the exotic single-estate white teas from China. Even their bags of Resolution Tea make a nice cuppa (and you can buy a box of 80 bags if you like it – available in the shop downstairs). There's a basic cream tea, with two scones, Yorkshire clotted cream and jam; a savoury tea with cheese scones; or a very reasonable full Afternoon Tea with sandwiches, scone and 'fancy cakes'. Or go for the Celebration Tea and throw in a glass of Madeira. Some local specialities: Whitby Gingerbread with Wensleydale Cheese; Yorkshire Brack with butter; Botham's biscuits.

35-39 Skinner Street, Whitby YO21 3AH

Tel: 01947 602 823
www.botham.co.uk

Opening hours

Closed Mondays (except July-August)
9.30am – 5.00pm Tuesday – Saturday
Closed Sundays
On Sundays in summer, and on Mondays in winter,
you can go to their other café in Baxtergate.

Coffee up the coast?

Tides

When owner Frazer moved to the area some years ago, he bought not only the Sandsend Stores grocer's shop (just up the coast from Tides), but also a small, dark hut on a patch of stone looking over the beach. This apparently used to be near the end of the line when steam trains ran to Sandsend, but more recently was a shop selling beach gear. He pulled the old hut down and brought in a local architect to design the superb blue wooden structure that now houses Tides coffee shop. They only opened up in April 2013, but with Frazer's barista background training, these guys know what they're doing. We were there on a perfect summer's day. I'd love to go back in a winter gale!

This must be the best coffee we had in the Whitby area. It's a rich, dark roast from Vinci Coffee. A good flat white, looking out over the incoming surf. What more could you ask for on a day at the beach? Cakes are baked locally by a lady in Whitby and brought in daily.

Sandsend, Whitby YO21 3SZ
Tel: 01947 893286
No web presence

Opening hours

9.00am – 5.00pm daily
They may close early if it's pouring down, though; and they can't guarantee these hours in January, February!

YARM

The River Tees loops round Yarm and it was still tidal when the massive flood hit town in 1881 – spot the extraordinary flood level markers on the Town Hall and above a garage down Church Wynd.

They had a meeting in one of the pubs on the High Street to discuss the building of the Stockton-Darlington Railway, but the big viaduct that looms over Yarm today was a different line, built some years later – still impressive, though!

Coffee?

The Mockingbird Deli

There's a real Italian feel to the menu, from the coffee (Caffe Saccaria, imported from near Ancona) to the pastries on display to accompany that cuppa. And since it's an Italian deli too, you have shelves of olive oil, pasta, coffee (of course) and other Italian delicacies. They do have scones and the occasional home-baked cake, too, but when in an Italian atmosphere…it's nice to do things the Italian way, we think.

Owner Martin Rodgers and his partner Helen are passionate about what they're doing and it really comes across in the way they work. Any free days Martin has, he's off to other coffee shops and delis in the area to see what he can learn. His background shows what a mix of talents he has, having worked in road-building for a local authority at first, he moved into sales for the fashion industry, which is presumably where he picked up his Italian connections that inspired him to open an Italian deli. He's a local lad – Middlesbrough FC supporter – and believes places like this should be a hub for the local community, which is why he is happy to support local artists and musicians.

18 High Street, Yarm TS15 9AE
Tel: 01642 913 357
Facebook: The Mockingbird Deli
Wifi available

Opening hours

8.30am – 5.30pm Daily (plus some evenings for music and light bites)

YORK

Highlight has to be a walk round the city walls for great views from every angle, and a chance to envy those lucky folk whose gardens back on to the walls.

The street names speak of its history: Colliergate, Gillygate, Jubbergate, Aldwark, Whip Ma' Whop Ma' Gate...Shambles is a favourite: formerly the street of butcher's shops; some of the meat hooks still hang over the cobbles.

York Minster, the largest Gothic building north of the Alps. Awe-inspiring from the outside if you can't face the entrance fee they charge these days to go inside.

Coffee or tea?

Spring Espresso

Spring Espresso have won awards for their coffee and for their tea, but if there were national cake prizes, they would almost certainly run away with them too, especially for their signature cake: Bourbon, pecan, apple cake. The coffee is top notch – they rotate the seasonal blends and have guest roasters in, but their main espresso is usually from the exquisite Square Mile in London. They're also into their tea, here, specialising in Chinese leaf teas from Canton Tea Company in Bristol, which deals directly with plantations in China. And in 2013 they were awarded Best Tea in the UK by the Beverage Standards Association.

Steve and Tracey have transformed a former York newspaper office into a bright, cheery espresso bar that combines old and new almost seamlessly. The wooden furniture comes from a 17th century mill in Bradford – take a look under one of the tables and see marks made by workers as they progressed along a job. And these two are great examples of how to make a complete career change if coffee or tea is your true passion: Tracey used to work in the health service; and Steve served in the air force, where he was an RAF photographer for many years (hence the excellent photos on their website).

45 Fossgate, York YO1 9TF
Tel: 07779 294 149
www.springespresso.co.uk
Twitter: @springespresso

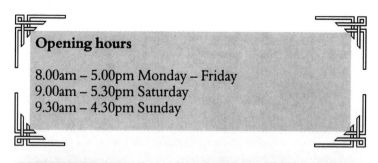

Opening hours

8.00am – 5.00pm Monday – Friday
9.00am – 5.30pm Saturday
9.30am – 4.30pm Sunday

The Perky Peacock

The coffee in this place is top quality. They get their basic espresso roast from Origin Coffee in Cornwall, but usually have a guest roast on offer, too – it was the delicious Peter James (PJGourmet) from Ross-on-Wye when we dropped by and they can make that with filter or any of the regular espresso drinks. Cakes are baked by owner Nicola's Mum, so you know you're in good hands there as well. There was lemon drizzle and Victoria Sponge on the counter for our visit, but the cakes rotate regularly.

The Perky Peacock surely lives in one of the quirkiest buildings on this North Yorkshire tour. It's in a tower by the mediaeval Lendal Bridge over the Ouse which was a toll bridge in the old days, but was also the tower into which dead bodies would be hauled when found in the river. Don't worry, the coffee shop is well above the water line, though during the Ouse's regular floods, staff have been known to be marooned here when floodwaters climb the first steps of the Tower. Fantastic spot to watch the water below or, if you have an outside table, spy on the people of York as they file by on the bridge above.

Under Lendal Bridge (Station side of the road and river), York
www.perkypeacockcoffee.co.uk
Wifi available

No toilets – nearest at the station or over the bridge and to the left in the library.

Opening hours

7.00am – 4.00pm Monday-Friday
9.00am – 3.00pm Saturday-Sunday

Tea?

The Hairy Fig deli and café

Owner Sue Hardy used to travel a lot in her earlier career and wanted to bring back some of the special foods and drinks she experienced to her local community in York. She set up the deli six years ago in what used to be an antiques shop and then the tea room in a former book shop. She found the enormous Indian tea urn at a local car boot sale; the tables and chairs in the café are made from driftwood.

Now this is what I call a good cup of loose leaf tea. The house blend is fantastic; a real pick-me-up blend of Darjeeling and Assam. Tea is bought in from a 200-year-old family firm in London. Cakes are baked in-house and delicious: we had the lemon and coconut, but there was also chocolate, Amalfi lemon and poppyseed; and a fat-free cake too. There's a cream tea (great value at under a fiver) with scone, butter, clotted cream and local jam. In the deli you can buy the tea or coffee you have just tasted, or go for some of their exotic looking olive oil or balsamic, some dating back 100 years!

In summer there's more seating out the back, in front of the grand Merchant's Hall or on the lawns. But worth waiting if they're full inside.

In summer there's more seating out the back, in front of the grand Merchant's Hall or on the lawns. But worth waiting if they're full inside.

39 Fossgate, York YO1 9TF
Tel: 01904 677 074
www.thehairyfig.co.uk

Opening hours

9.00am – 5.30pm Monday – Saturday
10.30am – 4.30pm Sundays (April to December only)

INDEX